M000290179

The Quill of the Chase

JAMES BYNUM

Paintings by Robyn Bynum

Charleston, SC
www.PalmettoPublishing.com

The Quill of the Chase
Copyright © 2021 by James Bynum

All rights reserved

No portion of this book may be reproduced, stored in a retrieval system, or transmitted in any form by any means–electronic, mechanical, photocopy, recording, or other–except for brief quotations in printed reviews, without prior permission of the author.

First Edition

Hardcover ISBN: 978-1-64990-722-6

I dedicate this book to my family, to

Forrest Fenn (R.I.P) and to all my fellow searchers.

Santa Fe Man

A Santa Fe man was growing quite old,
So North he went to hide him some gold,
How far he went remains to be known,
Some say to a land they call" Yellowstone ".

They say the "chest" is ten inches square,
All can look, but lookers beware,
Because this ole man is sharp as a tack,
He hid all the gold and he never looked back.

Nine clues he gave to us as a path,
Sounds simple to me, I'm doing the math,
Thirty minutes have passed since the clues I began,
Done figured out this Santa Fe man.

I'm packing my bags to go get the gold,
That poem was nothing, like what I've been told,
heading up north where the buffalo's roaming,
Up in the northwest part of Wyoming.

I arrive at the" secret" place that I've found,
Jump out of my truck, took off with a bound,
Climbed up to my spot where the water is high,
I looked for the blaze, but started to sigh.

It was then that I realized, without any doubt,
The poem was much more than I figured out,
It fits many places around this great land,
My "hats off to you" that Santa Fe man.

Many roads I have traveled, how long will it last?
Don't really know but" I'M HAVING A BLAST"
While I travel across this beautiful land,
I'll never again doubt the "Santa Fe" man.

The Chest

A chest I was made, from an elegant mold,
Many years ago, I'm really quite old,
By a craftsman hands, and the visions he had,
He took his time, one patient young lad.

He put on my lid, and gave me a latch,
Then picked out the nicest key in the batch,
Then lined me with wood, so beautifully bold,
To carry the book, of days that are old.

Those days are over, my missions anew,
Now I hold gold, and fortunes for you,
I've been hidden, for you to come find,
By an old man, who's one of a kind.

The silence surrounds me, as I sit all alone,
Hoping someday, to have me a home.
you'll open me up, as soon as you find,
What's held inside, will frazzle your mind.

Rubies, diamonds, sapphires so blue,
Gold galore, double eagles too,
But of all the things, that will catch your eyes,
The grandest of grand, a very small prize.

A silver bracelet, turquoise beads in a row,
Made by an Indian a long time ago.
To return to a man, with a smile on your face,
Thanking him for" The Thrill of The Chase ".

I'll wait for you, in silent repose,
How long will I wait? nobody knows.
But I will be here the day you arrive,
And fall to your knees in total surprise.

Enjoy the things, you see on your way,
The rivers, the mountains, the clouds far away.
I'm wishing you the absolute best,
Come find me I say, from your friend," THE CHEST " .

The Man in The Mirror

I looked at a man in the mirror,
And much to my mirrored surprise.
I leaned to him and got nearer,
I saw a sad look in his eyes.

His brows were silver and aging,
His eyes had feet of a crow.
Who is this man that I'm seeing?
He looks so withered and old.

I ask my new friend in the mirror,
In return, does he see the same?
Come on, lean in, get closer,
Is time the culprit to blame?

In silence, the man in the mirror,
Stared with that desperate same gaze,
To me his message was clearer,
Than the wrinkles upon his sad face.

I turn my back, to my new friend,
Goodbyes are so hard to say,
I turn at him, with a soft grin,
Then sadly, I just walk away.

James Bynum

Turquoise Buckle

Turquoise is the maiden stone, of many upon this earth,
A perfect blend of green and blue, when polished shows it's worth.
This stone was used by ancient man, for healing and for show,
How long ago this first began, no one really knows.

Turquoise holds a special power, for anyone who believes,
Clamp it tightly in your fist and feel that ancient breeze.
Blowing in the past of those, who lived upon this land,
Oh, the power in that stone, you hold within your hand.

Some turquoise beads were placed, on a bracelet in a row,
By an Indian who felt the breeze, many years ago.
Now it sits within a chest, filled to the rim with treasures,
But it's the turquoise, not the riches, where you will find your pleasure.

When the chest is finally found, and the lid is surly raised,
No doubt the look upon their face, will be astonished and amazed.
Ancient breezes will start blowing and Forrest he will chuckle,
Because the ancient past will speak to him, through his turquoise buckle.

Native Voices

Wrath fell upon a noble clan,
Where greedy men once sought.
Enraged by this new foreign man,
They vowed to give them naught.

Bows held in, their mighty hands,
With guns approaching fast.
They knelt upon the river sands,
Their battles here at last.

Through tempered eyes the shots they rang,
Through faith the arrows flew.
Their future on this battle hangs,
On this fight that now ensues.

Blue coats left their speedy mounts,
With arrows in their breast.
Natives lay in mighty counts,
Red holes within their chest.

Homemade wooden arrows,
Couldn't match the greedy guns.
To save more blood and sorrow,
Surrender had now begun.

The chief within this noble clan,
Standing in the sands of red.
Tear in his eye, spoke to his men,
His echoed words were said.

He gazed across the mighty land,
Spoke midst the winter weather.
"From where the sun now stands,
I will fight no more forever".

Old Santa Fe

I'm packing up my bags today, to head for Santa Fe,
Heading for the mountains, where I can roam and play.
Forrest gave his challenge, in which I proudly took,
Maybe I can get his pen, upon my favorite book.

The desert it is calling, I hear the mountains too,
Listen very closely, they're also calling you.
Though my drive is long, I'll cherish every mile,
When I reach old Santa Fe, I know I'll softly smile.

It's filled with ancient spirits, that lived there long ago,
Me I want to talk to them, to find out what they know.
Maybe they will whisper, of how it was back then,
Maybe I'll have a vision and see my ancient friends.

My confidence is high, and my face now has a glow,
It's time for me to leave now, time for me to go.
Maybe out in Santa Fe, I'll see you on the trail,
I know that I'll find treasures, even if I fail.

I doubt that you will read this, but Forrest if you do,
I'm living my adventure, all because of you.
I know I speak for all, we wish you all the best,
But most of all we thank you, for your mighty golden quest.

Orange Sky

The orange from the setting sun, mirrored on this placid lake.
Highlight distant mountain peaks, calm without a wake.
No breeze to spoil its beauty, no sounds are heard at all,
I'm deep within the solitude, as the evening sun it falls.

In thought my mind it wanders, Gazing in the golden sky,
Searching for the answers, up there so very high.
My time it quickly passes, the orange darkened fast,
Stars begin their peeking, in the sky so large and vast.

The beauty in this evening, I hold it dear to heart,
Another perfect ending, before tomorrow starts.
I have so many questions, for the orange sky above,
So tomorrow evening I'll be back, just doing what I love.

Poker Mouse

Jdiggins I'll tell you a story that's true,
Believe it or not, just out of the blue.
While sitting in my big comfy chair,
I had a feeling, someone else was right there.

I heard a sharp noise, then heard it some more,
I raised from my chair, headed straight to my door.
I opened it up, to see a surprise,
That mouse just stood there, with his beady brown eyes,

Beside him sat, his suitcase of red,
He asks so politely, to borrow a bed.
I welcomed him in and offered some food,
This mouse was polite, not the tiny bit rude.

To me he looked, familiar at bit,
Crashing my brain, as we talked where he sits.
He said that he came, from Cali so far,
Rode on his thumb because he hasn't a car.

He talked and I listened, as good friends should do,
He said while in Cali, he ran into you.
That's when it hit me, I remembered him well,
The trap hit my thumb and oh how it swelled.

Poker with friends and he scurried about,
Peeking at cards, then shouting them out.
That game I remember, yes quite well,
The fun that we had, our stories to tell.

While watching the mouse, as he steadily ate,
I asked him his name, he said it was Nate.
Then reaching inside, his suitcase of red,
That's when he looked, at me and just said.

How about a game, of poker my friend?
While grabbing a deck, with his sneaky ole grin.
I told him I'd play, if jdiggins would too,
No problem he said, then he headed for you.

The little old mouse, he passed on my bed,
With his little red case, that's when he said.
Well, it's back to Cali, I'll thumb it again,
He's off to go get you, for poker my friend.

So, listen for him, to knock on your door,
If you're up for some poker, we'll play it some more.
Then out of my door and into the night,
Nate my ole friend, then walks out of sight.

Transition to Spring

The bottom of the Hourglass is getting heavy,
But the white crystal sands fall ever so slowly.
The smell of the mountains coming alive is soon,
Birds will nest, Rivers will run freely with new water.

Warmth of the sun upon rock ledges will warm small chipmunks.
Gentle breezes from the south will be dominant again.
To carry the scent of blooming wildflowers,
The forest will come alive.

And flourish with the beauty it beholds.
Take the time to sit upon a log,
Close your eyes, smell and listen,
Feel the warmth upon your face.

Listen to natures song being sung,
While life begins anew, Spring has sprung.

Work of Art

Frost upon a mountain meadow,
Stars give way to morning light,
Off in distant, an elk that bellows,
Bald eagles take their morning flight.

A river flows, with ice on edges,
Gently to a lower ground,
Sheep stand high upon the ledges,
Like mighty monuments, looking down.

Alone within this perfect place,
The solitude warms, my chilly start.
With a peaceful look, upon my face,
What a treasure it is, God's work of art.

What They Do

A taste of pure forgiveness, was wet upon his lips,
A heavy load was carried, with pain from cracking whips.
One knee upon the ground, to rest a tiny bit,
Stones were flung by many, while others yelled and spit.

Armored men were brutal, they forced his every step,
Lookers by the hundreds, which many bowed and wept.
His will was truly tested, his strength wore down to none,
Up the hill he grunted, each step up one by one.

Two crosses were before him, a hole between the two,
His mother wept while watching, nothing she could do.
Laid upon his cross, nails drove through hands and feet,
Then stood up in the hole, his lips could barely speak.

Blood upon his face, both hands and feet the same,
His dry mouth it then opened, his words they softly came.
He looked up to the heavens, the sky above was blue,
"Please forgive them father, they know not what they do."

Quicksand's of My Time

While looking through old photos, with those whom which I care,
I notice how quick I'm aging, a silver lines my hair.
I feel as if I earned them, each and every one,
A silver hair for every year since my life begun.

I'm Looking at a photograph, when I was noticeably young,
Standing on our wooden porch, sticking out my tongue.
I notice in our yard, parked by the water well,
Dad's 47 Chevrolet, I thought this truck was swell.

There are many pictures, through the thickets of my life,
From cruising down the boulevard, to the wedding with my wife.
But as I proudly stare at them and talk of all the times,
That home now is grown up, covered over by the vines.

My running slowed down to a walk, a slow and steady pace,
My wrinkles have overtaken, the smoothness of my face.
But age will not deter me, I'll let my happiness shine,
Even though my feet are stuck, in the quicksand's of my time.

A Note to Cancer

You came into my body, not welcomed here at all,
I did not ask for you to come, for you I did not call.
Since your here, you must be warned, God is on my side,
There's no place in my body, that you can run and hide.

Let's not waste a minute more, let's get this battle started,
For I have not a tender soul, nor am I tender hearted.
I'm not fighting just for me, I'll fight for many more,
Who's lives you slowly crept into, I'll even up the score.

Through the many harden months, with you I have fought,
Not willing to give in to you, the victory that I sought.
My strength, faith and love of life, grows stronger every day,
Someday I'll be rid of you, I bow my head and pray.

I see your getting weaker now, my victories almost here,
Just to know your evil's gone, I know I'm going to cheer.
You have taken many lives, many that I know,
Now it's time for you to die, time for you to go.

I just received the grandest news, my doctor he did say,
That you have left my body, died and went away.
I drop my head, close my eyes, "Thank you God" I say,
For helping me with my battle, and with me all the way.

Many now are fighting, with the evils that I tell,
Fight with every ounce in you, and send CANCER
Straight to Hell.

A Warrior's Pledge

I promise as a warrior, within our noble clan,
Till death I will proudly fight, protecting sacred lands.
My courage I will show, with each new rising sun,
While fighting off the evils, I will never turn and run.

The stripes upon my painted face, the dark around my eyes,
Honor those who flew before, in spirit to the sky.
Smudge me now in smoke, I am ready to defend,
With my life I will guard you, until my very end.

Aching Soul

A snowflake drifts upon the air,
In the silent mountain night.
Upon a journey to nowhere,
Until it ends its flight.

Followed then by thousands more,
Until the ground is white.
With winter knocking on the door,
It is a cold and gloomy night.

Nestled in the mountain trees,
A cozy cabin sits.
Its smoke drifts in the winter breeze,
Its windows dimly lit.

An eerie silence bellows,
No sounds are heard at all.
No bugles from the fellows,
No nighttime mating calls.

The cold within a winter's night,
As snowflakes softly blow.
Can make a hurting heart feel right,
And sooth an aching soul.

Creekside Home

The year is 1540, as I sit upon this stone,
I'm lost within the memories, of my creek side tiny home.
A fire it blazes gently, smoke rises in the air,
It lingers through the valley, drifting to somewhere.

My home is made of rawhide, tanned by mommas' hand,
Wrapped around the poles, papa cut across this land.
But now they're just a memory, but it warms my chilly nights.
Until I go to see them and take my final flight.

The sun is setting lower, light dims within the west,
Orange shining boldly, beyond the mountain crest.
My day it slowly closes, I lay down on some skins,
I drift away in memories, of this home that I am in.

I dream about my childhood, so many years ago,
I dream about the winters, us kids out in the snow.
I dream about my first bow, my papa made for me,
I dream about my first love, "River Running Free".

I dream about my momma, with papa standing near,
I dream about their voices, again upon my ears.
I dream about my friends, already who have flown,
But most of all I dream, about my creek side tiny home.

Believe in You

Believe that you can do it, whatever it may be,
In time you will meet your goals, trust me you will see.
You and only you, walk on your trail of life,
My friends you must believe, in each and every stride.

Friends your trail is short, time will creep away,
Through life's given path, you will proudly find your way.
You will someday stop, arriving your trails end,
All your trail behind you, believe in yourself my friend.

Things out there await you, on trails within your soul,
Are you a true believer, to find them as you go?
Possible things can happen, just believe and let it show,
Focused on your dreams, so hit your trail and go.

Forever

In the year of 1877, amid the winter snow,
The Nez Perce fought their battle, in the land of Idaho.
They settled in the foothills, the army came with stride,
Some fled into the mountains, a wooded place to hide.

Others stayed below, to fight for sacred ground,
Through the snow they heard, shots from all around.
For many days and nights, the Nez Perce fought with pride,
Nez Perce blood was spilled, many Nez Perce died.

Soon they were surrounded, by armies of white men,
Within the bitter cold, their winter wait began.
Blankets they were few, children died from cold,
Chief Joseph knew his lands, they'd no longer hold.

Surrender was before him, he speaks within his clan,
He Tells them they will live, safe on distant lands.
He says to them while walking, along the frozen river,
"From where the sun now stands, I will fight no more forever".

The Light

Who goes there? Covered by the night,
Show yourself I say and step into the light.
Behind the dark of shadows, a coward place to hide,
Be brave and come I say, stand here at my side.

I gaze into the darkness, a glimpse within the night,
To see a shadow image, approaching to the light.
My thoughts they run astray, I bravely stand my ground,
The calm of night is silent, no eerie little sounds.

Into the light it enters, now just as brave as I,
To my knees I fall, a tear swells in my eye.
Standing there before me, such a peaceful sight,
An angel with her halo, my angel of the night.

Sent from Above to guard me, from evil lurking near,
Her voice was softly spoken and soothing to my ears.
She says her job is over, the danger it had passed,
Then flew off in the darkness, came and left so fast.

My angel brought a comfort, there in the black of night,
She bravely came to see me, she stepped into the light.
Whatever is in the darkness, whatever sounds I hear,
I'm not the least bit worried, I know my angel's near.

Desert Stars

The desert holds the secrets, of many moons ago,
Of those who lived within it, the lives of Navajo.
The year was 1620, the sun was on the fall,
Night was fast approaching, its shadows loved by all.

A fire it softly flickered, it's smoke it gently rose,
Beside it sat a worried, man of Navajo.
His fingers locked before him, leaned over to a slump,
Gazing in the campfire, in silence on his stump.

In a room within the Pueblo, was his wife of four short years,
Pregnant and in labor, with helping elders near.
Time slowed to a crawl, the sun had crept away,
Behind the distant mesas, to end this desert day.

Sounds they could be heard, her painful sounds deploy,
A reminder of the last time, he lost his precious boy.
The tiresome hours past, there by his lonesome fire,
He prayed into the stars, for help from someone higher.

The desert air was chilly, the moon was looking on,
The sounds of pain then ended, so suddenly was gone.
To his feet he rises, he gazed into the sky,
And there beneath the desert stars, he hears his daughter's cry.

Addition by Ronald Lee (RonnyLee) Oliver

A wail so young and tender, yet surely Loud and strong.
Then the laughter of the mother, mixed with sobs along.
Tears of joy were flowing, both inside the room and out.
Both pride and Grateful thankfulness, filled his heart throughout.

A Ship Within A Bottle

A ship within a bottle, it is held by tempered glass,
Kept from the open waters, a sea so grand and vast.
Resting on its pedestal, it dreams of distant shores,
But stuck within its bottle, its waves are never more.

Though once this mighty ship, it sailed the oceans wide,
Before its voyages ended, now trapped alone inside.
A world it once discovered, with wind upon its sails,
Now is just a memory, just stories it can tell.

Someday its glass will shatter, and winds will gently blow,
It will sail upon the waters and carefree as it goes.
Off into the sunset, on journeys bright and bold,
To sail where winds may take it, to ports the future holds.

Life is but a bottled ship, our journey waits inside,
Waiting for our vessel, to sail on gentle tides.
Don't sit upon still waters, don't wait on future winds,
Break your glass and sail, on your journeys deep within.

Ancient Skies

Along a flowing river,
Alone in midnights shiver,
He knelt and wept.

Feared what the darkness brings,
The healing chants did sing.
His wife fought as she slept.

Sounds of a newborn cry,
Filled the chilly sky,
Sounds of little grace.

His prayers sent to above,
To save his only love,
Or take her place.

His eyes filled with despair,
His heart overflowed with care,
Tears they fall.

Then chants they quickly cease,
Now worried doom or peace,
An Elder call.

Then through the tipi door,
There on the padded floor,
She smiles at him.

Upon their mother's chest,
His newborn daughters' rests,
Yes, two of them.

Speechless in his stance,
Eyes fixed in a trance,
Overflowed with love.

His answered prayer was sent,
There to his family's tent,
From the chilly skies above.

Way Up There

Alone I rest near dancing flames, in thought of years ago,
Mesmerized within its sight, the comfort in its glow.
The warming rays are soothing, a crackling now and then,
As if it's speaking to me, the sounds of way back then.

Like me the natives sat, close to their dancing flames,
Wrapped in their woven blankets, mesmerized the same.
The Navajo are special, their people stand apart,
Unlike a lot of others, they live from in their heart.

Gazing in my dancing flames, a Navajo's voice I heard,
Her softened voice I listened; I cherished every word.
She tells me of a time, so many years ago,
A blizzard fell upon them, the winds were bitter cold.

Pressured now by hunger, their food was running low.
The hunters could do nothing, blinded by the snow.
She said they gathered round, a dancing flame like mine,
And ask unto the heavens, his help just one more time.

She said her night was cold, she mostly lay awake,
Planning for her travels, for when she met her fate.
When morning it arrived, she heard some Natives cry,
She ran outside and noticed; sunshine filled the sky.

Deer were in the distant, hunters grabbed their bows,
Another year survived, through blinding winter snows.
She says goodbye and leaves me, alone I sit and stare,
She's taught me that my problems, have answers way up there.

Your World

Darkness hides a shadow, lightness shows its shape,
Wine hangs prematurely, on vineyard vines of grape.
Sun it lays its head at night, in morning it will rise,
Love within your heart, will shine through caring eyes.

Newborn baby crying, turns old in later years,
Lonely bells of silence, ring loudly in your ears.
Midst all your learning days, wisdom finds a way,
Springtime winds will blow, bringing thunder on the way.

Your life is charging at you, just like a running bull,
Make your wine with grapes, until your glass is full.
Share a passing smile, while sipping from your glass,
Enjoy your world around you, before it becomes your past.

His Brush

At rest upon this mighty rock,
These mountains are so grand.
It slows my ticking earthly clock,
To gaze across this land.

A silhouette before me,
Of peaks so far away.
A perfect place to see,
The dawning of new day.

The sky above is waking,
Awoke by morning light.
Artwork in the making,
Oh, such a peaceful sight.

The air is calm around me,
No breeze it moves at all.
I hear a lone Wapiti,
Sound out his mating call.

Special times like these,
Stored in my memory bank.
Are truly here to please,
I sure know who to thank.

Rays streak across the distant sky,
Past mountains in the far.
Then focused in my morning eyes,
The last but shining star.

A perfect morning for me,
I rest not in a rush.
To watch Gods artwork changing,
And the stroking of his brush.

Life's Driftwood

Life's a piece of driftwood, once stood on distant shores,
A monument in time, lives on for evermore.
When oh fate befalls, upon the mighty tree,
Storms of life will ravage; limbs fall in the sea.

Carried to the vastness, alone to drift about,
Molded by the waters, adrift with no way out.
To rest upon a distant shore, a lonely sandy beach,
Though Wet and waterlogged, each one is unique.

For each of us are different, molded by our life,
While drifting on life's ocean, as time it passes by.
When you reach your shoreline, all wet and faded out,
Thank oh God above, for letting you drift about.

I am Navajo

I am the leaves upon the trees,
I am the soft and gentle breeze.
I am the earth beneath your feet,
I am the sky in which you see.

I am the sun with warming rays,
I am the clouds that drift away.
I am the water within the creeks,
I am the snow on mountain peaks.

I am the eagle in the sky,
I am the sound within his cry.
I am the animals wild and free,
I am the plains without a tree.

I am the mountains rising high,
I am the valleys low and wide.
I am the rainbow with colors bright,
I am the stars within the night.

I am Navajo

Lilhunter's Clock

You say your mom, she has no clock,
For in the chase, she'll never stop.
That may seem so, for when you look,
But she pens of time, within her book.

She's using something, within her reach,
Not just in mind, not in her speech.
Lilhunter, I bet you know,
What makes her tick, what makes her go?

Now listen close to words not said,
Her clock is not, just in her head.
Because of you, her heart does tick,
A mom's a mom, through thin and thick.

Lilhunter, your mom is warm and true,
Listen to her heart, while it ticks for you.

Cosmic Knowledge

While cruising in my capsule, in the year of 3010,
Looking for anything, that belonged to ancient man.
The cosmic sun shines bright, I'm looking all around,
Then it quickly caught my eye, a reflection on the ground.

I lowered my capsule at the place, I seen down on the land.
Hoping to find something old, left by historic man.
I raised my door and stepped on out and started to look around.
And there it was just lying there, half covered in the ground.

I picked it up and couldn't believe, in my hands so glad,
Gazing there in disbelief, I held an ancient ipad.
I jumped into my capsule and hurried back to my slip.
The ipad I inspected it, while biting on my lip.

I pushed the button, at the bottom, and then to my surprise.
It came on, brightly shined, right there before my eyes.
An ancient man named Focused, speaks of a hidden chest of gold.
And all the knowledge they had back then, man he sounds so old.

He wrote upon this little wall, I hold within my hands,
He speaks about the wisdom, they spread across the lands.
I sit here with his ancient iPad, I hear a cosmic blast,
I don't need the wisdom; knowledge is of the past.

Riches I'll have, but no knowledge I'll need,
Thank you Focused for your writings, and for planting my golden seed.

Distant Drums

Boom 1-2, boom 1-2, sounds of distant drums,
I hear them in the twilight, at the setting sun.
The elders in my village, smudge young braves in smoke,
While they're dancing proudly, not a word is spoke.

As I sit upon this cliff, their fires Below they flicker,
I too was once a brave, but now I'm getting sicker.
Many snows behind me, no snows I'll see ahead,
Right here on this cliff, I'll rest until I'm dead.

I look up to the heavens, I thank the mighty God,
For many years I've walked, upon this precious sod.
My wife I've said goodbye, she's pregnant with our child,
I thought that I could last, to see her painful smile.

The sun has finally set, with distant fires aglow,
I know my time is over, it's time for me to go.
I lean back in a crevice, I look up to the skies,
In the sound of distant drums, I hear my baby's cry.

This Old Brown Hat

My mind reflects to years ago, beneath a lodge pole pine,
To an incredibly special memory, of George a friend of mine.
The sky above it sparkled, all stars were shining bright,
The air was crisp and cold, a perfect Wyoming night.

The fire it slowly crackled, with embers on the rise,
I was lost in conversation, beneath the starry sky.
My coffee gave me comfort, within an old tin cup,
But not as much as George, who gladly filled it up.

Buffalo skulls beside us, a brown hat upon his head,
Then George removes it slowly, and this is what he said.
"Friends like you are few, so many come and pass,
My hat I'm sure will fit you, like water to a glass".

He placed his hat upon my head, it's brown with heavy wear,
Our friendship grew much stronger, within the chilly air.
Coyotes in the distant, the smell of burning pine,
Nothing could be better, here with a friend of mine.

That was many years ago, he's no longer on this earth,
This old brown hat, to me at least, is priceless in its worth.
For many years I've worn it, in honor of my friend,
But what lies in its future? When my time someday ends.

The future I've decided, I'm not waiting till time is up,
Again, I'll sip my coffee, from a weathered old tin cup.
Beside a lazy fire, with its embers rising red,
I'll place my old brown hat, on top of Shiloh's head.

So, he can wear it proudly, as I have many years,
It's seasoned for the journey; it'll help with future tears.
This old brown hat is special, oh the stories it could tell,
While placing it back upon my head, in my eye a tear it swells.

Saving Grace

Many, many years ago, in the mountains of this land,
There roamed a group of Arapaho, guided by one man.
They went into the mountains and left their prairie land,
To explore across the ridges, with knives and bow in hand.

Looking for a special place, told by their elder men,
A waterfall with powers and healing waters grand.
Three of them were sick, they knew their time was near,
Their leader leads them onward, not showing any fear.

For days they roamed the mountains, not wanting to give in,
Weak and tired they climbed, nearing their life's end.
Then one of them fell to his knees, as if to go no more,
While kneeling he could hear, the waters faintly roar.

With all his might he struggled, back to his feet again,
The strength within the Arapaho, shown within this man.
Along the creek they traveled, and much to their surprise,
Around a bend they seen it, right before their eyes.

It was the special waterfall, spoke of the elder men,
Standing at the bottom, the mist it sprayed on them.
The sick knelt to their knees, prayed to the mighty spirit,
Praying to the" Great One ", knowing he could hear it.

Then they waded in the pool, created by the falls,
While standing in the water, they hear an Eagles call.
Then totally submerged, their bodies in that place,
In silence under water, they heard their saving grace.

Then they traveled downward, back to their prairie tribe,
With many years before them, their sickness left to hide.
Life within the Waterfall, felt by these Arapaho,
Forever will be cherished, everywhere they go.

So next time you're out hiking, and see a waterfall,
Think about the Arapaho, while watching water fall.
And if you're sick and ailing, go find your special place,
And wade off in God's water and hear his saving grace.

The Orchard

Walking through an orchard, the rows are straight and neat,
Up above the sky is blue, cut grass beneath my feet.
The wind is gently blowing, the branches slowly wave,
Perfect day to gather fruit, that mother nature gave.

Then I noticed up ahead, the edge of a water canal,
One lone tree just standing there, damaged by a plow.
It was pushed off to the side, as if nobody cared,
To me it looked majestic and its fruit was also spared.

I crawled down to the water's edge, my basket in my hand,
From here I'll gather all my fruit, that is if I can.
Standing below the branches, they wave above my head,
Reaching to grab an apple, that was shiny and deep red.

Perfect day of solitude, I enjoyed beneath that tree,
In a ditch, bound with fruit, just waiting there for me.
My basket full I headed back, down that perfect row,
The apples in my basket, seemed as if they glowed.

Lessons that I learned that day, I'll pass them down the line,
So, others too can enjoy their walk, through their orchard of sunshine.
Just because you stand alone, not in a neatly row,
Doesn't mean you're not a color, of Gods all mighty rainbow.

If your ever in a ditch and your feeling all alone,
Think about the fruit you bear, like that I carried home.
Yes, my day was perfect, no cloud within the sky,
But not as perfect as the taste, of my fresh made apple pie.

Placid Lake

When standing near a placid lake,
The mind can drift away.
Winds subside and calms the wake,
Of waters back in the day.

Life is memories, making more,
Slow down your hurried pace.
Down beside a peaceful shore,
Only then you'll know this place.

Then upon this mirrored lake,
Can you see your distant past?
You see the life you make,
See reflections in the glass.

Your hourglass is heavy,
True but don't mistake.
Reflection from the levy,
Upon your placid lake.

The sands will soon be gone,
Calm your waters wake.
Still your life upon,
Waters of your placid lake.

The Warning

Way out in the desert, so many years ago,
There lived a tiny tribe, of peaceful Navajo.
One that lived among them, his name was Running Bear,
He lived in peace and harmony, without a single care.

He was a brave young lad, of only seventeen,
His hair was long and black, his body short but lean.
Winter was approaching, the north winds gently blow,
Camped along a creek side, where water slowly flows.

One evening he was resting, upon a Mesa top,
He gazed across the land, deep within his thoughts.
That is when it happened, a spirit came to him,
A vision of a girl, just floating in the wind.

Her words were softly spoken and pleasant to his ears,
She said that she's been gone, for many, many years.
She warns him of some danger, just lurking south of there,
So, he could warn his people and he could go prepare.

She tells him of some Spaniards, new into this land,
With silver on their spurs and guns within their hands.
Then her vision left, just blew off with the wind,
Running Bear turned and ran, to warn his fellow man.

The news it quickly spread, to each and every one,
They knew they were no match, to the strangers with their guns.
They packed throughout the night, moved to the Mesa top,
Within the morning sun, below them Spaniards stopped.

Horses rode in circles, they looked upon the ground,
They knew it was a camp, but not a soul around.
The Spaniards rode on north, vanished around the bend,
The vision then returned, upon the morning wind.

Running Bear gave his thanks, to life so long ago,
Warning of the danger, for which he didn't know.
Her vision it then faded, like smoke within the sky,
His people gathered around him, to watch her spirit fly.

Then slowly down the hillside, the Navajo they descend,
Running Bear stays to gaze, across the desert winds.
The morning wind is brisk, it brushed across his cheek,
He looks down from the Mesa top, at his people by the creek.

Without the Wealth

While chasing lures, of elusive gold,
Search within, your soul that holds.
Look upon, your inner shelf,
The treasures there, within yourself.

Live in peace, your victory's prize,
Your heart will see, through caring eyes.
You'll find the lures, within yourself,
And rich you'll be, without the wealth.

Playing in The Sand

High upon a desert knoll, I gaze across the land,
A Fog lays in the valley, along the Rio Grande.
The year is 1460, I am a Navajo,
I listen to the spirits, speaking through my soul.

The sun is gently rising, no clouds within the sky,
I hear the native birds, begin their morning cry.
I'm visited by a spirit, a girl of long ago,
She says her name is Ajei, named for her special glow.

As the morning lingered, Ajei spoke to me,
She tells me of her life, and how it use to be.
She says she lived below, along the Rio Grande,
And as a child she played, within the rivers sand.

One day while she was playing, a child of only ten,
The sky began to darken, a storm was moving in.
The winds began to blow, while lightning flashed afar,
She knew that she must leave, her homes not very far.

When running to her home, Ajei starts to cry,
That is when she seen it, fall from the darken sky.
A tornado twisting wildly, with debris that flew about,
Headed for her home, all she could do was shout.

She hit her knees and prayed, "God save my family home",
As quick as it appeared, it rose and then was gone.
When Ajei reached her village, with everyone untouched,
Again, she looked above and thanked him very much.

Then her spirit left me and alone I sit again,
Thinking about her words, my newfound spirit friend.
While looking at the Rio Grande, many feet below,
The sky began to darken, the winds began to blow.

Ajei she has warned me, lightning starts to flash,
I thank my native friend, from a way off distant past.
Before I leave, I gaze, down at the Rio Grande,
That is when I see her there, just playing in the sand.

Campfire Stories

While out in the mountains, searching for gold,
At the campfire, where stories are told.
Waiting your turn, while everyone tells,
Of Their daily adventures, and dusty ole trails.

Your patience pays off, now your time has come,
To tell them your story, of a day full of fun.
You start your story, as all searchers do,
At warm waters halt, sounds perfect to you.

All ears are listening, while each clue you pass,
Pausing sometimes, for a sip from your glass.
The campfire is burning, while you're poking about,
The embers are rising, then quickly go out.

Your story's about over, your down to the blaze,
All eyes are upon you, steady fixed and a gaze.
Just when you're ready, to tell them about,
A loudly ole fart, done found its way out!

Laughing and joking, from all your friends,
You gather yourself, to tell them the end.
No one is listening, lost in the moment,
Nothing to do now, just sit there and own it.

The campfire is shining, an extremely low light,
But That's not the only blaze, that's gone for tonight.

42's Hand

When the dealings are over, all cards on the table,
You will show your hand 42 and win if you're able.
All bluffing is over, and all betting now finished,
With your ace up your sleeve, your bank will replenish.

Do not stand at the table, like wanting to leave,
Other players might have, an ace up their sleeve.

A Single Tear

In a teepee, On a desert Mesa, in a dry an arid land,
The chief he softly talks to spirits, while raising up his hand.
Praying for the mighty peace, to rest upon his people,
Spaniards came into their lands, forced prayer on Spanish steeples.

Before the jingle, of silver spurs, came into their space,
The Indian of the desert Mesa roamed this beautiful place.
High upon a pointed cliff, they would sit with inner peace,
Now they rarely leave the sight, of their elder chief.

The Spaniards came in numbers, slowly taking over their lands,
Many a brave's blood has spilt, across these arid sands.
The spirit has spoken to the chief, words carried in the wind,
" You're fighting a mighty battle; I know you cannot win".

The chief he raises to his feet, walks out the teepee door,
Calls a meeting of all man, says" we will fight no more".
Braves, squaws and little ones, sat quiet in their space,
They saw a single tear swell up, roll down the ole chiefs face.

The chief he turns and walks away, no other word was said,
Back into his teepee, lays on his deer skin bed.
From that day on they followed, the dictates of white man,
But not a drop, of Indian blood, has dripped upon the sand.

Choices that the old chief made, were extremely hard to do,
But maybe there is a lesson here, for the likes of me and you.
Sometimes we should swallow pride, for the benefit of others,
All of us now share these lands, so therefore we are brothers.

Next time you are faced, with the decision of war or peace,
Remember that one single tear, that rolled down an old chief's face.

Focused on Happiness

Remember through life's journey,
My words I pen to you.
Friends listen closely to me,
You will live a life renewed.

Only then you'll feel as,
Live as you can be.
Once you release your dim past,
Be happy, wild and free.

Happy awaits to shine through,
See how it can bless.
You won't regret the days you,
Focused on happiness.

Dreams of Fall

Dreams adrift, like crimson leaves,
Float upon a crispy breeze.
Chased by hands, so highly raised,
Determined, caring, where dreams lay.

If ever rest, upon the ground,
A dream will rot, not ever found.
But dreams that fall, within your palm,
Like magic turns, chaos to calm.

Chase on my friends, with hands held high,
And catch your dreams, now floating by.
Then cup your hands, and gaze within,
Smile at your dream, then chase again.

Forking Branches

Sometimes we stop and wonder.
What makes a life so rich?
We gaze at others yonder,
Spend years behind this glitch.

A searching soul should listen,
Lifetime passes fast.
Searching things that glisten,
For things to hold a mass.

We've had our years of chances,
Had not the eyes to see.
All the forking branches,
Along our family tree.

Golden Sunsets

Staring at the sunset, his brush within his hand,
A master of the canvas, known as Thomas Moran.
Setup on the riverbank, Green River I am told,
A sunset in Wyoming, midst every shade of gold.

The river in the foreground, a bird is flying low,
Reflections on the water, add a subtle glow.
Way off in the distant, rock cliffs standing tall,
In this golden hour, just posing for us all.

Gently in his brush strokes, on canvas lay his oils,
He Captured Mother Nature, no blemishes or spoils.
The sun was getting lower, few clouds within the skies,
Thomas, he continued, gold colors in his eyes.

When he finished painting, dark was closing in,
Upon his bearded face, he wore a golden grin.
To some real beauty lies, in petals of a flower,
To Thomas Moran it lies, within that golden hour.

Thank you for your travels, there with your brush in hand,
Thank you for your paintings, created for all man.
Thank you for the images, full of nature's power,
Most of all I thank you for, sharing your Golden Hour.

The Grave Robber and The Nun (part I)

Many, many years ago, out in the desert west,
A stranger kept a timepiece, tucked within his vest.
He roamed from town to town, over many dusty trails,
Looking for a graveyard, where honest men had fell.

He'd sneak into a graveyard, under darkened skies,
While townsman slept in slumber and rest their tiresome eyes.
He'd walk into the graveyard, a shovel in his hand,
One by one he'd dig, into the desert sand.

Stealing goods from those, who lay in peaceful rest,
Things like that ole timepiece, tucked within his vest.
He was an evil man, who lived his life alone,
Always on the move and robbed things for his own.

One night while in a graveyard, the moon was shining bright,
A vision walked up to him and slowly came in sight.
Amazed at what he seen, he froze there in his tracks,
A nun was wearing white, while he was wearing black.

As she spoke her words, were soft within the night,
She tells the stranger how, just how this isn't right.
With eager ears he listened, with a warmness in his chest,
The nun continued speaking, just telling him what's best.

Then her vision faded, like smoke within the wind,
In disbelief the stranger, knew that this must end.
He covered up the graves, slowly one by one,
And sat beside the gate, to wait for morning sun.

When the sun had risen and the townsmen moved around,
He raised up to his feet and strolled down into town.
It was a Sunday morning, the sky was blue and bright,
Guided by the nun, he seen within the night.

The church doors were wide open, townsmen filtered in,
He too just walked among them, to cast away his sin.
On a hand carved bench of wood, he sat so ever still,
Thinking of the night, he spent upon the hill.

From that day on the stranger, never dug again,
For him, those days were over, he'd leave the world of sin.
So, if your ever thinking, about the evil's you have done,
Think about this story, of the grave robber and the nun.

The Grave Robber and The Nun (Part ll)

The stranger sat in silence, he felt the nun was near,
As he listened to the sermon, just echo on his ears.
A sermon on forgiveness, no matter what the deed,
From that day on the stranger, he tossed aside his greed.

The stranger left the church, back into morning sun,
He gazed upon the hill, where his new life had begun.
For days he traveled westward, then topped a gentle rise,
He stopped to look upon, a town before his eyes.

The townsmen were all framing, a barn from piles of wood,
The stranger rode down to them, to help them if he could.
Proudly they accepted, he joined them on that day,
Grateful for his presence, they thanked him for his stay.

For weeks he labored with them, as children ran around,
Proud of his new riches, not buried in the ground.
With the barn completed, he passed by every man,
Nodded as he smiled, shaking each and every hand.

The morning it was young, the wind was calm and still,
Then the stranger noticed, their graveyard on the hill.
He rode up to the graveyard, where a weeping woman sat,
He reached above his head and removed his dusty hat.

Then rode on up the hill, in a trotting steady pace,
A warmness in his chest and a smile upon his face.
Just Thinking of the nun, who wore her robe of white,
He knew one day he'd find her and thank her for that night.

Then down the dusty trail, alone the stranger rides,
Off to find the next town, beneath the western skies.
One by one he'd visit, until his work is done,
All the while he's searching, for a precious holy nun.

Golden Pond

In the year of 1350, alone I drift about,
Rejected by my people, for they have kicked me out.
They say there's evil in me and band me from the tribe,
My face it shows my sadness, with tears in every stride.

My Apache hearts been strong, all my twenty years,
In strength I will continue, I'll proudly hide my tears.
Alone within this desert, my days are very long,
Listening to the birds, while they sing their desert song.

There is no evil in me, my woman's heart is pure,
How did they see evil? That haven't any cure.
Alone I press on forward and with each passing day,
I kneel to watch the sunset, falling as I pray.

When I reached the foothills, I came across a creek,
Maybe it holds the answers, to everything I seek.
I traveled up the creek side, through willows bright and green,
Ahead the white cap mountains, most beauty I have seen.

My Apache feet are tired, and I can't continue on,
While traipsing through the willows, I find a hidden pond.
The sun was getting lower, so here I'll spend the night,
At daylight I'll continue, looking for my life.

As the sun is rising, the pond it has a glow,
I feel today is different, somehow, I just know.
Then I see a mother deer, there with her spotted fawn,
Watching as they drink, across the golden pond.

They jumped into the bushes, spooked by something near,
Then Apache voices, I faintly start to hear,
Then I see their faces, they were Apache bred,
They welcomed me to join them, in prayer I dropped my head.

They knew that I was coming, the spirits told them so,
Across the special waters, that held a holy glow.
For years I lived among them, welcome as can be,
For they did not see evil, when they looked at me.

Happily, I spent my days, they were not so long,
Living with my family, across the golden pond.
Just because your judged sometimes, knowing it's not true,
Don't give up, keep on living, your family waits for you.

Golden Wings of 9/11

Today the bell of freedom rings, for all our loved ones lost,
Today we remember the price, paid for an evil cost.
Why did it happen? what was the reason? questions always ask,
Answers we may never know, Lost forever in the past.

Now a mighty monument stands, forever in its place,
To remind us of their mighty smiles, they wore upon their face.
Husbands, wives, sons and daughters, Loved down to the core,
Brother's, sister's, aunts and uncles, loved forever more.

Take the time to pause today, let silence fill your ears,
Remember those whom on this day, left us with our tears.
For they are in a better place, forever to behold,
Flying with our God above, over the streets of gold.

Some day we will join them, in that mighty golden place,
To see their shining golden smiles, upon their golden face.
Until that day, honor those, who left on 9/11,
For now, they fly on angel wings, forever with God in heaven.

Forrest's Family

We came into this Chase, each and every one,
Ready for adventure, chasing dreams and fun.
Even though we're strangers, we're closer than you think,
When your help is needed, no one even blinks.

This family we are part of, grows stronger every day,
I listen to the blogs, and what the searchers say.
I hear it in their fingers, while typing here for all,
When danger really draws nigh, you're at the beacon call.

While Randy chased his dreams, adventure filled his eyes,
When he came up missing, the choppers hit the skies.
Others hit the Mesa tops, with boots upon the ground,
Vowing not to give up, until our brothers found.

As I watch this all unfold, from many miles away,
Wishing I could help you all, each and every day.
But distance is a factor, for many more like me,
But prayers will cross the distance, upon a bended knee.

When Randy came up missing, we all were crashing thoughts,
Chasing gold and fortune, sharing ideas we've got.
But I have noticed lately that no one speaks of gold,
Everyone is trying, to find Randy the cold.

As I type these words, my chest swells from within,
Proud of all the searchers, and the family that I'm in.
Forrest take a look around, this family you have built,
Because of you, we chase our dreams, you should feel no guilt.

As I finish up my words, I'll say it once again,
This sure is an amazing family, thank God you are my friends.

Melody

The winds of time gently blow, life's chime it plays a tune,
A melody a heart must play, beneath a lifelong moon.
In the sounds of ringing years, all notes they join as one,
Until the winds they softly fade, and your melody is done.

Then deaf upon the present ears, your volume turned to none,
Your soul embraced by lovely tunes; your journeys just begun.
In flight amongst the pillow clouds, a journey to home anew,
To share a lifelong melody, the tunes you bring with you.

Delighted in your journeys end, pure gates of solid gold,
Enter with your melody, for eternity be holds.
The angels chorus playing, your melody joins them,
In joyful sounds of heaven, your soul goes drifting in.

Mindy's Prayer

Mindy you're a special friend,
I know your feeling down.
Sure, I have a card to send,
Hope and care abounds.

You need to take a little time,
Get much needed rest.
Feeling will return and shine,
Better then to best.

My thoughts are there beside you,
Friend hear me as I say,
See you feeling down and blue,
You know I'm going to pray.

Sunrise in My Heart

Sun it cracks the mountain peaks, streaming rays of gold.
Past distant fir and rocky walls, it's colors bright and bold.
Alone high in the mountains, no gold could ever buy,
The riches in this moment, here in the mountain high.

With its grand ole entry, a new day boldly starts,
Feelings of much larger, emerge from in the heart.
A smile it cracks, a steady gaze, into the sky above,
Nearby sounds within the trees, a pair of morning doves.

The morning brightens slowly, the mountains come alive,
A lonely waking chipmunk, with eagles soaring high.
The rushing water hurries, as if to get somewhere,
While morning chill it rides, upon this mountain air.

No words can ever match it, no book can tell it right,
The mountain sky above, here in the morning light.
Replenished by its beauty, the natures morning glow,
One last look behind me, as down the trail I go.

Time to Rest

For years I've written on this blog, sharing words of rhyme,
To those who want to listen and give little of their time.
To those a real big thank you, for your caring words to me,
Just because I'm resting, doesn't mean that I don't see.

Many stories I have inside, which someday I will tell,
But now the ink is running low, inside my old ink well.
Many here upon this blog, I've known for quite a while,
To those friends I must say to you," Thank You" for your smiles.

Every trail within the woods, has an end somewhere,
Think about what you'd do, if your ever standing there.
To me it would be simple, I'd continue through the woods,
So, I can see that special place, where no man has stood.

There I'd sit alone, in the quietness of my soul,
Thinking about the past and spirits of long ago.
Here my trail has ended, so I will sit and rest,
To my many online friends, I'm wishing for you the best.

Within Your Wood

Within the wood, a voice is heard,
Softly spoken, it's every word.
Of memories past and yet to come,
Its rings tell all, years one by one.

Though dry and cracked, no leaves remain,
It needs no more, soft subtle rains.
The stories of, its yesteryear,
Now fall upon, our present ears.

Now breath, look and listen well,
To its days of glory, before it fell.
Learn its lessons, there where it lay,
Someday your limbs, will stop their sway.

Go now enjoy, your life of green,
Build your oak, with many rings.
So, when you rest, there where you stood,
They'll hear your voice, within your wood.

What You'll Find

Beside a lonely river, an old man sits alone,
Gazing in his campfire, in thought of days now gone.
Wrinkles on his saddened face, they tell his story best,
His life, his work, his family and how much he was blessed.

The dancing tiny flames, they reflect within his eyes,
While stars above they fill, the chilly mountain sky.
The sound of flowing water and the crackling of his fire,
Speak to him as if, they're spoke from someone higher.

The old man deeply thinks, of deeds throughout his life,
His goodness gave to others, his kindness during strife.
To this old man it measured, his life upon this earth,
Alone beside his campfire, he knew what he was worth.

He knew his time was nearing, his journey he could see,
He leaned back in the firelight, against a fallen tree.
And with his shaking pen he writes, a note to leave behind,
Then stuffed it in a mason jar, for someone else to find.

The sky above then added, a bright new shining star,
As his lonely fire reflects, upon his mason jar.
On a tiny piece of paper, the words he left behind,
"Good deeds won't go unnoticed; peace is what you'll find".

Moonshine Still

I know a man, who is making shine,
Chased by Feds, for quite some time.
Popcorn Sutton, is indeed his kin,
He comes to visit now and then.

To bring me gifts, delivered himself,
To place upon my cellar shelf.
But I am no nark, my lips are sealed,
I like his backwoods, moonshine still.

Natures Call

Beneath the autumn leaves I've slept,
Upon a bed of gold.
Thinking of my secret kept,
That natures gladly told.

Autumn air it has a chill,
While passing, leaves do fall.
Alone upon a wooded hill,
I listen to natures call.

Virgo Stars

Late into a Virgo night, fresh grass beneath my head,
Just gazing at the stars above, no single word is said.
Cause on a dark and starry night, a mind can travel vast,
To the long-forgotten times, you cherished in the past.

The sliver of a crescent moon, shines softly in the east,
The banquet table of my thoughts filled with this starry feast.
At least a billion stars I see, bright shining in the night,
Each one has a purpose, while showing off its light.

My mind it drifts back to a time, when I was only ten,
Wishing I was sixteen, how little I knew back then.
Then when I was sixteen, I wished for twenty-one,
Cause that's when it was legal, to have adult like fun.

Now I gaze into the stars, and many years have passed,
Now I wish for time to slow, and not to go so fast.
Just laying here, looking up, into the sparkling sky,
A shooting star, with tail so bright, went shooting quickly by.

I know I'm granted just one wish, upon a shooting star,
It doesn't take me long at all, for what I'm wishing for.
I close my eyes, to make my wish, upon this starry night,
Silence still surrounds me; my thoughts will be alright.

I wish for all the ten-year old's, all across these lands,
Don't wish away your childhood, enjoy it while you can.
Cause someday in the Virgo stars, you'll gaze into the night,
And cherish those childhood memories, riding on your huffy bike.

Three Doors

Three doors wide open before me,
the choices I must make,
Not as simple as it sounds,
which door that I must take.

They all are doors to somewhere,
They're ready to step within.
But only one door leads the way,
to where I can use my pen.

Title to Your Gold

I see you've went alone so bold,
I too have done the same.
Wishing I wasn't quite so old,
To play this crazy game.

The canyon it looks mighty deep,
And the waters hot as hell,
It's all too far to walk for me,
My knees they slowly swell.

What the heck's, a home of Brown?
I'm old but brave you see.
I hope the ends, just nigh and down,
It's taking a toll on me.

I need no paddle, my creeks to high,
But I'd use it as a crutch,
My heavy loads, my aching thighs,
I've never hurt so much.

Wise you say. I'm worried now,
My smarts lost in this haze,
I've got to find your blaze somehow,
I've had my better days.

While looking quickly down below,
I see where my quest will cease,
That's much farther, than I can go,
To rest my throbbing knees.

Regain my breath and off again,
No tarry scant for me,
Not much farther, this game I'll win,
Then poof, I'm gone in peace.

Why is it, that I must go?
It's beginning to be a chore.
I think I'll wait to grab your trove,
My body's crazy sore.

I guess I've done it, tired and weak,
So, hear me Mr. Fenn,
Listen now and hear me speak,
I think I'm giving in.

Will someone send a chopper in,
I'll resume, when hell is cold,
My effort it can wait till then,
For the title to your gold.

The Coal Miner

At 4:00 A.M. I wake, I try to make no sounds,
I work within a coal mine, deep within the ground.
My lunch pail it is ready, with a pie dish on the top,
I'm running kind of late and have no time to stop.

Arriving at the coal mine, I walk into the door,
My coveralls are frozen, wet from the day before.
My body it will thaw them, so I head on to the mine,
Another day below, to earn an honest dime.

I grab my carbide light and my trusty ole pickaxe,
While standing at the mine shaft, I take a last look back.
I walk into the blackened mine, long before there's sun,
While others ride the train out because their shift is done.

When I reach the bottom, a small shaft waits for me,
On my knees I crawl, my carbide shines to see.
While laying on my side and with my pick in hand,
I chip away at coal, as steady as I can.

My mind it drifts away, to help me fight the cold,
I remember in my childhood, the stories mama told.
The day's that I spent fishing, with Dad along a creek,
My children up above, their kisses on my cheek.

The day it slowly passes, my arms are tired and sore,
I proudly keep on chipping, the boss man he wants more.
When my day is over, a coal car waits for me,
I ride up to the surface, so bright that I can't see.

My workday it is over, I head back to my place,
I walk into my front door, with smiles upon their face.
My children they are waiting, all sitting on the rug,
They jumped and run up to me, with open arms and hugs.

To me my day was worth it, because they depend on me,
My Time now with my family, we're happy as can be.
Tomorrow I will rise, before the morning shine,
And do it all again, down in that cold, cold mine.

The Move

I've been living in a crow tribe, all my twenty years,
I've seen my people smile; I've seen them shed their tears.
I'm packing my belongings, tomorrow we must move,
Water it is scarce, and we haven't any food.

We'll bundle up our teepee's, when we take them down,
And drag them to another place, a wet and hallow ground.
The buffalo here have grazed, across these parries wide,
Now we must go find them, just so we'll survive.

With the early morning light, I gently raise my head,
Raise up to my feet and in hunger roll my bed.
I look out of my teepee, my people move about,
I go and help an elder, to take their fine home down.

I look up to the heavens, the sky above is blue,
A great day to be moving, I know what I should do.
Now the sun is higher, our village it is packed,
Upon a gentle rise, no one's looking back.

Over hills we travel, and through the valleys wide,
Looking for the buffalo, wherever they might hide.
Way off in the distant a dark cloud starts to form,
Lightning strikes the ground, one single little storm.

All day long we traveled, my people they are tired,
We stop and make a camp; we started several fires.
When the sun comes up, we'll do it all again,
Hoping for a place, that we can call the end.

For days we traveled onward, we top a grassy rise,
In the valley before us, I can't believe my eyes.
The buffalo they are grazing, at least two hundred head,
I know our journeys over, this place we make our beds.

With our teepee's raised, we'll call this place our home,
As long down in the valley, the herds of buffalo roam.
I speak up to the heavens, and thank our mighty spirit,
With thunder in the distant, I know that he can hear it.

I live within a crow tribe, in a vast and spiritual land,
A rainbow in the distant, wouldn't change it if I can.

Yellow Daffodils

Why is it that the daffodils, are always blooming first?
Eager for the springtime, to let their colors burst.
You see them blooming just about, everywhere you go,
Then later you will see them, Beneath the white of snow.

Springtime it draws closer, each and every day,
Soon the snow on daffodils, will surely melt away.
The green will start emerging, daffodils will stand tall,
The looming grays of winter will leave till after fall.

Listen to the sounds, while the springtime song is sung,
Birds begin their nesting, a place to raise their young.
Of all the flowers in the spring, scattered across these hills,
None are more inviting, than the yellow daffodils.

My Doli Pot

I'm walking through the desert, of north New Mexico,
Looking for some signs, of life so long ago.
The sky above is blue, I'm in a dried-up creek,
That is when I see it, just resting at my feet.

It looks to be a pot, half submerged in sand,
With figures bold and black, drawn by ancient hands.
Excited I kneel down, and with my tiny brush,
The soil around the pot, I remove not in a rush.

The midday sun is warm, with sweat upon my brow,
I wondered how it got here, I can't imagine how.
That is when it happened, a spirit spoke to me,
She told me of her life and how it use to be.

She says her name was Doli, she owned the lovely pot,
And many, many years ago, the day was very hot.
She came down to the creek, for water they could drink,
Then danger came upon her, in fleeing let it sink.

Then her spirit left me, as quickly as it came,
Standing up I thanked her and called her native name.
Then with a gentle hand, I lift the fragile pot,
Amazed in disbelief, at the treasure that I've got.

As I leave the creek and head back to my home,
My mind it drifts away, what a perfect day to roam.
And With my pot in hand, that Doli made herself,
To honor her I'll place it, upon my favorite shelf.

One Memory Away

Alone on a bar stool, while the couples they dance on the floor,
In memory of your smile and our beautiful days once before.
This dim lit ole bar room, it brings back my memories of you,
Like your fun silly smile, suddenly out of the blue.

And our trip to El Paso, beneath your sombrero of red,
Our laughing and joking and all the fun things that we said.
Or our ski trip to Aspen, in the mountains all covered in white,
Alone by the fireplace we'd talk, deep, deep into the night.

With a shot in my hand and raising it high, this toast is for you,
For the memories you gave me, before you left with somebody new.
In this Smokey ole bar room there's one thing, that I'd like to say,
Even though you are now gone dear, your just one memory away.

Forgive

Our journey is not measured, by what we see but feel,
It's sought within the solitude, alone so quiet and still.
Within a heart's forgiveness, sown for only then,
A journey in yourself, to rise from deep within.

There's a magic in the silence, a healing kind of sorts,
Locked within your fortress, your lonely solemn fort.
Breech the walls around it, escape and start to live,
Escape into the solitude, forgive, forgive, forgive.

Gentle Wind

The other day while walking, a voice I softly heard,
An Indian spirit came to me, I listened to his words.
He also had a vision, I could see him standing there,
His narrowed face was young, midst the long black hair.

It's been 800 years, since he walked this land,
He shows me in his vision, an item in his hand.
He said he worked for weeks, carving it from bone,
Now that it was finished, he'd take it to her home.

It was a special fetish, to wear upon a string,
When held up to your ear, you heard the bluebirds sing.
He carved it for a special girl, he met 2 years before,
She lived across the lake, upon the other shore.

He says his given name, they called him Gentle Wind,
Because winds were softly blowing, when his life began.
His friend I see in visions, she's beautiful as can be,
Her black hair gently blowing, beneath a cottonwood tree.

His spirit tells me of a day, the snow had gone away,
He took his little fetish, to give to her that day,
In his handmade canoe, made of sticks and hide,
He settled in and paddled, towards the other side.

When he arrived upon her bank, she was waiting there,
To meet him on the shoreline, a feather in her hair.
For hours they sit and talked, but when he headed back,
She was also paddling, his fetish around her neck.

In the middle of that lake, he asked her for her hand,
She gladly said she would, he was a happy man.
Together they rowed along, then reached the other side,
Across the sands he walked, with his someday bride.

Before his spirit left me, he said he had a blast,
He thanked me for my time, While I listened to his past.
He said while we're out hiking and doing our own thing,
If we'd listen to the Gentle Wind, we'd hear their bluebirds sing.

Fiery Band

Throw at us your fiery band,
And sweep across our precious land.
Remove the things that once was ours,
And leave us with our memories scared.

If that's the best that you can throw,
There's something else you ought to know.
Yep, we are safe, though all is gone,
We'll rise again because we are strong.

We'll build again and start anew,
Bigger, stronger, just for you.
Don't waste your time, another year,
We fear you not, we'll be right here.

You're just a hated, evil fire,
But your no match, for our life desires,
For when you die and your smoke is gone,
We'll live on, in our mountain home.

The Promise

Deep within a jungle, a lonely meadow waits,
Covered by the grass, those men who met their fate.
A stream is quickly flowing, carefree as it goes,
It turns into a waterfall, falls in the mist below.

The rushing water rumbles, in the silence of this place,
So peaceful and remote, a special kind of space.
A chopper it approaches and lowers softly down,
Until its runners meet and touch the grassy ground.

A soldier exits quickly and steps upon the ground,
To keep his daily promise, to this waterfall he had found.
Upon the edge he rested, till time for him to go,
Tossing stones of thank you, into the mist below.

The soldier he then rose, to head back to his home,
But in the grass, he tripped, for he was not alone.
Upon an aging stone, was a Frenchman's name inscribed,
A marker for a soldier, where in the tall grass died.

A promise was delivered, one soldier kept his word,
One soldier stayed behind, a voice that's now unheard.
The chopper it then lifted, slowly set to go,
A salute from one brave soldier, to another who rests below.

Cold, Cold Halloween Night

With Halloween approaching, and time was running out,
I was prepping for a party, with ghost that fly about.
A few more things I needed, to make my party right,
So, into town I drove, on a moonless chilly night.

While driving down a dirt road, about 5 miles from town,
My car just up and quit, the engine it shut down.
The lights were burning bright, just shining down the road,
Without my heater working, my car was getting cold.

Then a gentle fog, came slowly rolling in,
The longer that I sat there, my light were getting dim.
While looking for a flashlight, around inside my car,
Without one I was thinking, I wouldn't get very far.

I found a tiny flashlight, it's beam's not very bright,
But with it started walking, in the foggy, chilly night.
About a mile on up the road, I looked back at my car,
In the fog it looked like, a dim lit distant star.

With my tiny flashlight, which now was getting dim,
Along the ditch I walked, the road it made a bend.
This is when it happened, a noise within the woods,
I quickly shined my light, just looking if I could.

While shining in the wood line, I seen some glowing eyes,
Frightened and alone, I hurried up my strides.
The eyes they followed with me, not even trying to hide,
Then I see some more, there on the other side.

I stopped within the roadway, and slowly shined around,
Eyes were all around me, not making any sound.
The lump within my throat, was large as it could be,
This is when it happened, the eyes all lunged at me.

Each one had a growl, loud within the night,
Me I couldn't move, overtaken by my fright.
Then the lights came on, flashlights everywhere,
All my kids surround me, just laughing as I swear.

With reflectors on their shirts, that looked like shining eyes,
Me I hung my head because I fell for their surprise.
Then around the bend, lights from our old farm truck,
My family they are pushing, their everlasting luck.

The night was very chilly, though Halloween was near,
Everyone was gloating, with their victory in my ears.
Me I sat there quiet, my ideas were burning bright,
Planning how I'd get them back, on a cold, cold Halloween night.

Desert Smoke

The sun is large and setting, a softly east wind blows,
Another desert day comes quickly to a close.
I take my tiny twigs and place them in the ring,
To build a fire for others, to dance around and sing.

The year is 1560, my how time it flies,
Many, many moons, have passed before my eyes.
The wrinkles on my face, they tell where I have been,
Also, where I'm going, upon my final end.

The sun is now asleep, my fire it blazes high,
Embers quickly rising, up in the desert sky.
I'm joined now by others, my journeys almost here,
I hear our Native chants, echo in my ears.

Our chief he walks up to me, his hands upon my chest,
And in our native tongue, a prayer to me he blessed.
My heart is feeling heavy, my breathing slow and weak,
I turn and walk away, too tired to even speak.

I take a trail that leads, up to the Mesa top,
And many, many times, upon that trail I stopped.
My final journeys ended, as high as I can be,
I see my fire a burning, I hear their chants for me.

I kneel down on both knees, I reach up to the sky,
And tell the mighty spirit, it's time for me to fly.
A vision of an eagle, it soars above of me,
To fly me to a home, that's waiting there for me.
A warmness overcomes me, I raise up from the ground,
And join that mighty eagle, together fly around.
I hear no sounds below me, my people as they spoke,
But as I fly off in the sunset, I smell the desert smoke.

Coyote Calls

Way out in the desert, before the modern man,
A Navajo sat calmly and gazed across the land.
High up on a Mesa, with a moon so full and bright,
The desert breeze was blowing, so gentle in the night.

The stars above they glistened, a coyote seldom calls,
Below her was her home, with thick Adobe walls.
The breeze it softly moved, her hair so long and black,
Beside her was a deerskin, all tied up like a sack.

Within the sack were special, handmade tiny rings,
A gift to leave the spirit, in thanks for many things.
Made by her own hands, carved from seasoned bone,
In thought of those before her, who now are dead and gone.

She reaches towards the heavens, beneath the desert moon,
She prays up to the spirit, she knows her time is soon.
But now was not the time, she leaves her deerskin sack,
Then down the moonlit hill, she slowly heads on back.

To her the moon holds secrets, a journey yet to take,
It holds a love so lasting, a reminder what's at stake.
Then as she reached the creek side, standing by Adobe walls,
Beneath a distant moonlight, a lone coyote calls.

The Brown

The morning it came quickly, my alarm just woke me up,
Time to grab my fishing gear and head out to the truck.
I drive down to the river's edge, while others lay in bed,
With thoughts of landing trophies, dancing in my head.

I park my truck and walk around, to let my tailgate down,
I hear the flowing river, in twilight making sounds.
The fog is kind of thick and the air it has a chill,
I'm slipping on my waders, ready to show my skill.

I grab my lucky vest, that was passed down from my dad,
I grabbed my net and fly rod and the favorite flies I had.
When I reached the water's edge, I knelt down on one knee,
I sent a prayer of thanks, for special days like these.

The sky is getting brighter, I slowly wade on in,
Then I worked my line out, my fishing just began.
As I cast into the fog and gently place my fly,
I try to reach a boulders edge, there near the other side.

Then I finally placed my fly, a tiny bit upstream,
Disappearing as I twitched it, my line began to sing.
With my fly rod bending down, my arms were in the air,
I knew I had a big one, my biggest one I swear.

After a mighty battle, I finally wore him down,
As he rolled up beside me, I seen he was a Brown.
Yes, he is a trophy, I grab him with both hands,
I look up to the sky and I thank God once again.

With both hands in the water, I hold this mighty fish,
From his mouth I take my fly, too tired to even splash.
As I gently hold him and move him back and forth,
Slowly he revives, through his gills the waters forced.

I look into his weary eyes, I feel as if he knows,
Slowly I release him, then up the river he goes,
As I watch him swim away, I know I done him right,
Next time when we meet, I know he'll give a fight.

Seasonal Cabin

The sky of blue, will soon fade away,
Replaced by a somber, skies of Grey.
Sunshine it hides, embarrassed still,
Winds from the north, with its howling chill.

Ole man winter, at his cabin retreat,
Under his blanket of snow, he quietly sleeps.
Months they pass, while he rests all alone,
Enjoying the drafts, of his new winter home.

Then came a knock and a knock once again,
A Voice from outside, saying "please let me in ".
He opened the door, of his new drafty place,
The sun it shined brightly, upon his cold face.

Standing beyond, his now opened door,
The Man of spring, with his sunshine galore.
Ole man winter, must leave his cold room,
Spring he moves in, with all his blooms.

For a month or so, the beauty emerges,
The flowers they bloom and all life it surges.
Springs stay is short, like a quick moving clock,
Then outside his door, another heard knock.

Ole man summer, he came to retreat,
With him he brings, his suitcase of heat.
The Creeks go dry, the hot days are long,
Heard in the night, crickets singing his song.

A knock once again, summer answers the door,
It's Fall standing there, with his baggage galore.
My time to stay, he says with a grin,
And with him he brings, a slight chill in the wind.

With Colors abound, in the trees very high,
Against the subtle, light blue of the sky.
Soon they'll be nothing, bare trees all alone,
Another knock on the door, Ole Man winters came home.

The Phantom's Light

In darkness lonely phantom waits,
Wails heard throughout the night.
Awaiting for a passing soul,
On its journey to the light.

Eager for the journey,
Like many souls before.
But knows within the darkness,
He lives forever more.

The phantom in the darkness,
He wails a painful cry.
Pleading for the mercy,
From the light within the sky.

He seen a new soul coming,
A glow of subtle light.
The phantom sat in silence,
From him no sounds of fright.

The light approached the phantom,
A warm and steady glow.
Says softly to the phantom,
It's time for you to go.

Together on their journey,
With darkness left behind.
Flew off into heaven,
A home that always shines.

Roy

Sitting by my campfire, just staring at the coals,
Embers quickly rising, flashing as they go.
A blanket across my shoulders, a chill is in the air,
My mind is free to roam, all I can do is stare.

My mind it drifts away, to a time so long ago,
Like me a man is sitting, in a gentle mountain snow.
Staring at his campfire, it seems so strange you see,
I feel as if he's looking, just staring back at me.

Then he speaks into the fire, his voice I clearly hear,
He says his wife is pregnant, the time is very near.
The elder women of his village, they go into his teepee,
Into the fire he talks, he hears but he can't see me.

He says that this will be, the first for each of them,
Nervousness in his voice, I give a subtle grin.
Then through the fire I hear his wife, I know the time is here,
I hear the happy voices, of the elders as they cheer.

While his baby's crying, he speaks into the blaze,
And thanked me for my time, to help him through that day.
He said the time has come, to name his newborn boy,
He asked me what my name was, I said that it was Roy.

He pauses for a moment, then into the blaze he speaks,
What kind of name is Roy? What does it really mean?
Then says it doesn't matter, it's fitting for his boy,
Proudly he will bear it, a Cherokee we call Roy.

As I stared into the fire, my friend he said goodbye,
I said how proud I was, but he seen it in my eyes.
As the fire dies down, the coals now softly glow,
I'm thinking about little Roy, a Cherokee from long ago.

Whiskey River

I'm addicted to a whiskey bottle, it's tearing me apart,
I'm Rafting down a whiskey river, I've broken many hearts.
Day by day I drift along, no oars within my hands,
No control where I drift, I know that this must end.

Soon this whiskey river, will pass through rocky walls,
This raging river will kill me, with its whiskey waterfalls.
I know I need to find a way, to make it to the shore,
And leave my bottle in my raft, to drift forever more.

My family I've neglected, my friends I've pushed away,
It didn't matter much to me if I had my bottle each day.
time has come, I'll take my chance, and jump from this crazy boat,
into the raging whiskey river, I'll swim to stay afloat.

No one can make me do it, the courage I must find,
And show my friends and family, I've left the bottle behind.
This whiskey river I'm floating in, will soon be of the past,
And with a jump I entered, the evil river with a splash.

I fought, fought and struggled, the whiskey had its hold,
I beat the raging whiskey river; on solid rock I hold.
Then Raised up to my feet, amazed at what I saw,
Downstream the river disappeared, over a whiskey waterfall.

The bottle I have conquered, alone and proud I stand,
From this day on I promised God, to be a different man.
My Family and friends await me, they worry that I have drowned,
But I can't wait to show them, the courage that I have found.

From this day on I promise myself, I'll never raft again,
Down that whiskey river, with currents made of sin.
If your floating on a whiskey river and your floating all alone,
Find your courage jump and swim, your family waits at home.

Trusty Ole Friend

I too jdiggins, I'm in the same boat,
Adrift on an ocean, just staying afloat.
The poems a current, no oars in my hand,
It carries me onward, thanks to the man.

Someday you'll see, a bird upon flight,
It'll lead you to land, where You'll welcome the sight.
You drift not alone, your drifting with friends,
Hoping someday, your ship will come in.

But first we must start, where the currents begin,
Keep looking for land, my trusty ole friend.
And if you drift, to that magical place,
Remember us your ole friends, with a smile on your face.

Peace

Listen, Hear the distant drums?
Preparing for when the morning comes,
Paint your faces, paint your horses,
Dance your fire rings, plot your courses.

Braves will live, Braves will die,
They'll fight the battle, on desert high,
To defend their lands, from those who take,
Life and death are what's at stake.

Mount your horse, the mornings near,
Grab your bow and grab your spear,
Chant along with distant drums,
Mornings here, the time has come.

The Chief he stands, with pipe in hand,
Chants they stop, each and every man,
They listen to his word so wise,
While tears they swell within his eyes.

" The time has come for peace of all man",
" No more bloodshed, upon this great land".
" Our fathers they died, so we can be free",
" No more pain, for you and for me".

Let us live on this earth with one another,
Call us you friends, call us your brothers,
And as the distant drums start to fade,
Look at the lives this wise chief saved.

No more bloodshed, no more grief,
live your life like an honorable Chief.

Desert Moon

The sun sets on the desert, darkens as it falls,
Coyotes in the distant, barking evening calls.
A Rattlesnake in hiding, it slithers from a crack,
Beneath a desert moon, with diamonds on its back.

Me I sit alone, upon a mesa's edge,
Staring at a full moon, to it I give my pledge.
I was born a Navajo, with pride deep in my veins,
And to this mighty moon, my pride is just the same.

I pledge to make a difference, each and every day,
In everything I do, and everything I say.
Looking at the desert moon, huge within the sky,
My eyes begin to water, tears they fill my eyes.

I also made this pledge, to someone long ago,
This pledge I still will honor, just as I told her so.
Within my arms she left me, my wife of 15 years,
While giving me a son, she died with happy tears.

Until I take my final breath, I'll remember all the times,
We sat beneath this desert moon and heard coyotes' whine.
This moon to me is special, a doorway bright and vast,
When I stare into it, I see her in my past.

Tomorrow is never promised, tonight may be your end,
Go and make a difference, I know you can my friend.
Look into your desert moon and make your pledge tonight,
Always do what's good and always do what's right.

Rising to my feet, my time has come to go,
Beneath a desert moon, this desert has a glow.
A rattlesnake just slithers off, a slow and steady crawl,
As I turn to leave, I hear, a hoot owls lonely call.

Crazy World

Today I walked out my back door,
To breath the morning air.
Like many other days before,
To enjoy what's waiting there.

I know you won't believe me,
But all I say is true.
The world outside was eerie,
I knew not what to do.

The sky was lovely green,
My lawn a deep sky blue.
The craziest thing I've ever seen,
The birds like cows they mooed.

My dog sounds like a horse,
My horses barked so loud.
An airplane above of course,
Flying backwards through the clouds.

Fall leaves were falling upwards,
The morning sun goes down.
I take a huge step backwards,
Amazed at what's abound.

Both hands upon my morning head,
My rooster starts to crow,
It sounds just like my truck of red,
While on its horn I blow.

Back into the house I ran,
It's a crazy world outside.
Back to bed, quick as I can,
Beneath my pillow hide.

I peeked into my windowpane,
In fear of what I've seen.
Awoke I yawned, outside it rained,
It was just a crazy dream.

Earthly Gold

A subtle breeze, a morning dew,
This trail alone, I walk.
Now relieved, my thoughts renewed,
As nature starts to talk.

Sun rays in the distant,
Skip past the mountain peaks.
The beauty in the instant,
By far the best in weeks.

More out there awaits me,
My eyes have yet unseen.
Beyond this lonesome valley,
Like riches to a king.

Someday I'll see the beauty,
That heaven surely holds.
Unlike a king, it means to me,
More than his earthly gold.

Free Wisdom

For wisdom comes in many forms,
Some much beyond our daily norms.
Through trial-and-error wisdom grows,
It has no limits, for this we know.

We begin at birth, our chalkboard blank,
Day by day, we grow and think.
Years they pass, our wisdom grows,
Our knowledge blooms, the more we know.

Still starving for, a wisdom treat,
Our mind it growls, more knowledge please.
Our hair turns white, as white as snow,
With still so much, that we should know.

My friends please listen, to what I say,
There's so much more, you can learn each day.
Don't just settle, for the wisdom you've got,
Just add more knowledge, in your own wisdom pot.

For someday when, your mind does rest,
You'll have the wisdom, to pass life's test.
Now grab a book and learn something new,
Don't miss the wisdom, that's waiting for you.

Life's Wisdom is free, now you make the call,
Enjoy your life, while learning it all.
I'll take my own challenge, until my days end,
And all that I learn, I'll share with my friends.

Blast from The Past

Sitting here reflecting, how my childhood was back then,
The Land of the Lost on TV, and the river sucked them in.
Let's not forget ole ET, and how his finger glowed,
Pointing at the moon above, as he spoke the words, phone home.

While playing with my GI Joe, and humming tunes from Mash,
I thought That I could save the world, before my chopper crashed.
Stretch Armstrong he was also, one of my favorite toys,
His arms would stretch forever, he was wanted by all the boys.

Atari was the first game, ever played on our TV,
Pong it was my game of choice, no one could ever beat me.
I must admit that I removed, stickers from my Rubiks Cube,
So, I could win a friendly bet, with my good friend Luke.

Then the music caught my ear, I listened to everything,
My favorite song was Moody Blues, by Elvis who was the king.
Then there's Michael Jackson, who invented the Moon Walk,
His dancing and the moves he had, would make the whole world talk.

I felt that in my kingdom, I was the mighty ruler,
Until I was told to spray the pads, of our rusted Water Cooler.
We did not have a Cadillac, we owned a Station Wagon,
Cause All us kids could fit in there, while fussing and a nagging.

Then came along the Pogo Stick, this thing it broke my arm,
Then the game of Simon, which never caused me harm.
Parachute Pants and Bell Bottoms, were the pants of choice,
Girls they wore the Go-Go boots, noticed by all us boys.

Some things that I'll not talk about, embarrassed still today,
Give me another twenty years, then maybe I will say.
I could keep on going, because my childhood was a blast,
Thanks for taking a trip with me, while I traveled to my past.

Close Knit Family

Life Has many different meanings, to those who walk this earth,
Is it time for you ponder, where you truly place your worth?
Not to fix on shiny things, things you cannot see,
it's about the life around you, and your close-knit family.

The time may come for you someday, for you to look and see,
Treasures bold just sitting there, waiting to see your glee.
You traveled many, many miles, and life is passing by,
Seek yourself deep down inside, it never hurts to try.

It's the feeling within your heart, where the treasures truly lay,
About the way you live your life, until that final day.
The life you live upon this earth, reflects the way you die,
Treasures are there for everyone, who gives an honest try.

You have one tool within your chest, dig deep and you will see,
Have faith in God, and thank him for, your close-knit family.

Desert Christmas Day

In the year of 1560, in a desert of the west,
There stood alone Apache, with beads upon his chest.
A blanket on his shoulders, a feather in his hair,
He gazed across the desert, staring to nowhere.

Winter was upon him and Christmas Day was near,
The smell of smoke surrounds him, burning fires were near.
Deep in thought he stood there, his mind it was adrift,
He pondered on a perfect thing, to call a Christmas gift.

With his mind made up, he walks back to the tribe,
Looking for a special place, to where his gift should hide.
Each day as they were passing, he'd walk off all alone,
And gently carve away, on a hardened weathered bone.

Then he took some shiny stones and shaped them into beads,
His hair would blow while working, from the chilly desert breeze.
Then he took a rabbit hide and cut from it a strip,
Upon it one by one, his beads he proudly slipped.

His necklace he had made, he wrapped within the hide,
And took it to his special place and placed it safe inside.
Christmas Day grew closer, he was patient as can be,
But ready to give his gift, to his wife of twenty-three.

Christmas in the desert, the day had finally came,
He Awoke her from her sleep and softly called her name.
Kneeling on his knees and with his gift in hand,
Awaken and surprised, she proudly took his hand.

She took his Christmas gift, with excitement in her eyes,
Carefully she rolled back, the wrap of rabbit hides.
Before her was a necklace, handmade by her man,
Around her neck she placed it, helped by his own hands.

This Christmas Day was special, out in the desert west,
He proudly gave her something because she deserved the best.
The snow began just falling, the children run and play,
'To her a perfect start, to a desert Christmas Day.

Cross to Bear

Fear not the lengthening shadow,
Embrace its slender stance.
Cherished by the memories,
Be proud you've had the chance.

Some choices were consuming,
Within you they were made.
For the better, crack a smile,
As you look upon your shade.

Please keep one thing in mind,
As beyond the clouds you stare.
Like you we all have choices,
We've got our cross to bear.

The Little Things

Look at all the little things,
Not noticed in your lives.
That's when freedom truly sings,
just listen with your eyes.

Tornado

Quickly I wake from silent slumber,
A flash of light with distant thunder.
Each one closer than the flash before,
Soon it will be knocking upon my front door.

I rise to prepare for what lies ahead,
So many things, they bounce through my head.
Gather the candles, without any doubt,
Cause during bad storms, my power goes out.

The rumble's much louder, than it was just before,
A crack, a Flash, I head for the door.
Open it up, to my surprise,
The lightning bolts dance across the dark skies.

The lights they flicker, they go off and come on,
I know that soon, they too will be gone.
What? The sound I'm hearing sounds like a train,
With Flashes of thunder, wind and the rain.

I fall to my knees, to God I do pray,
Please make this storm go farther away.
The windows they shatter, the rain comes on in.
Hoping and praying, this not be the end.

Suddenly I've wakened, with sweat in my hair,
Only to realize, the weather is fair.
Through the window I see, skies that are blue,
Another day starting, morning anew.

This nightmare it seemed as real as can be,
Or was it a prayer, Answered especially for me?

Chilly Winds

Spirits carried in the wind, of life so long ago,
Drift about among us, upon the breeze that blows.
Take the time to listen, to what they have to say,
Me I took the time, one hot bright sunny day.

While walking through the desert, alone I strolled about,
Not caring where I went, I knew my own way out.
I stopped to rest within the shade, beside a giant boulder,
The desert heat just faded, the breeze it got much colder.

That is when it happened, a spirit I could see,
A ghost like faded image, she walked right up to me.
Still, I sat and listened, to her every softened word,
A voice as sweet as heaven, best voice that I have heard.

She said she was a healer, she had a caring hand,
Many friends she's helped, throughout her native land.
Through sickness and disease, she was by their side,
Until the evil left them and gone away to hide.

We sat and talked for hours, my newfound spirit friend,
But as the wind died down, I knew our time has end.
And as she softly faded, into the desert air,
That is when I realized That I was never there.

When my eyes they opened, a doctor I could see,
Family gathered round, each they looked at me.
A miracle in the desert, they said it time again,
But I knew it was the healing, from my spirit friend.

Her spirit helped me through, the unforgiving odds,
I know that she was sent, from the one and only God.
Ever since that day, I've tried to find my friend,
Walking miles throughout the desert, in search of chilly winds.

James Bynum

Believe

Your fears must dwell, on dusty shelves,
Your dreams are plans, within yourself.
Live now Anna, your words ring true,
Chase your dreams and believe in you.

Deal Me In

I have seen your mouse, on my shoulder at times,
Smiling and happy, And talking in rhymes.
Though I didn't understand a word that he said,
I am sure that you know, cause your face is all red.

Off from my shoulder, quickly he ran,
Over to you, to tell you my hand.
Jdiggins you hold, a straight that is flush,
Royal of course, and keeping it hush.

So, this time I fold, your mouse makes me scared,
Throwing away, my sevens are paired.
So next time you send, your mouse on the race,
Try to hold back, the blush on your face.

This time it cost you, the pot is still small,
If not for your mouse, Ida given it all.
My other three cards, were all the same,
This time your mouse, has cost you your fame.

Let's deal them again, all cards anew,
There's Nothing like poker, with friends such as you.
"DEAL ME IN!"

Friendly Poker

I sat at the table, surrounded by friends,
Cards are all dealt, let the bluffing begin.
All faces kept straight, not cracking a smile,
All wanting the pot, out there in a pile.

I have four cards, and a joker of one,
I'm not going to show it, till the betting is all done.
Each player they bet, or check when it comes,
Their time to act, not showing their runs.

The "flop" has been shown, all bets are thrown down,
Next is the" turn" card, I'm showing a frown.
Others they notice, the look on my face,
They think I have nothing, the betting they "raise ".

Two pair that I hold, and a joker of one,
I'm matching their bets, not showing my fun.
Some players have folded, now two they remain,
The" river" card lands, last round of the game.

This time I bet, I could see in their eyes,
I push" all in", Their look of surprise.
One player has" folded ", the other pushed too,
Now, let's show the cards, starting with you.

A" straight" of five cards, ending in king,
I then show my" full house", my grin how it rings.
I drag the pot, with both hands as I say,
Listen real closely, it'll help you someday.

In the game of poker, a frown goes a mile,
In the game of life, reversed, It's a Smile.

My Mental Chase

While sitting on an airplane, reading a provided book,
A poem written by Forrest Fenn, I had to pause and look.
It talked about a treasure, hidden for us to search,
I was hooked from then on, it got me off my perch.

Since then, I've had many dreams, lying there in bed,
Many trips into the mountains, scratching at my head.
Now I see the words he wrote, they twist within my mind,
Trying to decode a poem, that's taking all my time.

Now I look at numbers, on signs along the road,
Could it be a hint to me, of Forrest's heavy loads?
This happens all the time, no matter where I go,
Other times I walk in circles, knee deep in the snow.

Some say I'm going crazy, in this golden chase I'm N,
Floating like leaves of autumn, upon a chilly wind.
Eye see where they are coming from, and wear I'm going two,
Butt most of all eye have made, friends as nice as ewe.

Eye will C ewe in the mountains, that's wear Eye will B,
Looking four a treasure, left their 4 ewe and me.
Win I'm finished looking, and I'm old and Grey,
Then put me N a mental home until my final day.

Navajo Pride

In the year of 1560, in a quiet and solemn place,
There sat a lonely Navajo, with sun rays on his face.
It shines upon the wrinkles, created by the years,
Smooth and aging skin caused by olden tears.

For many years he's walked, upon this precious sod,
And now he sits in peace, communing with his God.
His legs are very tired, his breathing soft and weak,
A softness in his voice, though he can hardly speak.

He hears off in the distant, the children as they play,
A place that he called home, before he walked away.
Not ever to return, he left and took his pride,
And found a special crevice, to which he crawled inside.

It's facing to the east, to catch the morning rays,
So, he can feel the warmth, within his final days.
His wait is finally over, the time has quickly come,
His God is speaking to him and softly calls his son.

He leans back in a crevice and looks up to the sky,
That is when he seen it, his spirit starts to fly.
Faintly in his ears, he hears a voice again,
Calling him to his home, that God has built for him.

Pdenvers Quarter Horse

My mind it has been crashing, a poem left for us,
Now I have my solve, so I'll jump a greyhound bus.
I feel I'm getting close now, I'm starting to prepare,
A rental car reserved, to get me here and there.

I have my trusty hat, stained from sweat and salt,
I'll wear it on my journey, to where warm waters halt.
Canyon down no problem, it's getting back that worries me,
With a load so heavy and with my weakened knees.

But I'll not count my chickens, at least before their hatched,
One by one supplies, from my list I scratched.
I must find a topo map, that shows me water high,
I guess I'll go to Walmart, deep breath and then I sigh.

My supplies are now gathered, just one more thing to buy,
That topo map at Walmart, I guess I'll go and try.
I drive down to our Walmart, it's just too far to walk,
I notice as I park, to the doors the people flock.

I grit my teeth and hang my head, walking towards the doors,
Quickly in and out, a map and nothing more.
As I reach the doorway, the doors they open wide,
I raise my head to look, as I stepped inside.

I know you won't believe me, but I will not tell a lie,
That is when I see it, something caught my eye.
Kids were gathered round, and some began to cheer,
Pdenver's on the "Quarter" horse, with a grin from ear to ear.

Off I Go

Beneath a hollow leafless tree,
In thought of times that used to be.
My upper teens, oh times were wild,
This carefree, crazy, hot rod child.

Then the 20's, they came so fast,
My toddler drank, from a Barney glass.
Then I blink, my 40's they slow,
But hey, where did my 30's go?

Then 50's come up, next in line,
I eat by 6, watch news at 9.
Beneath this tree, it finally hit me,
I can't slow down, just because I'm 50.

I jump to leave, the hollow tree,
There's so much more, that waits for me.
Now in my car, my blood it flows,
As I squeal my tires, and off I go.

Pueblo Dreamer

Many, many years ago, out in the desert sand,
There lived a tribe of Navajo, it was their home back then.
They carried water from a creek, at least two miles away,
So, they could mix the mud, to make their pots of clay.

There was a special Navajo, which lived within this clan,
With visions in his mind, to help his fellow man.
He was a distant dreamer, his thoughts ahead of Time,
Others often looked at him, didn't pay him any mind.

For days he carried water, and placed the pots just right,
And then one day he started, in the early morning light.
He'd dig a hole within the ground and pour some water in,
With his hands he'd mix the mud, until it suited him.

Others the just watched him, they thought he lost his mind,
They stared as he erected, one thick wall at a time.
With four walls proudly standing, he left so they could dry,
He went and built a ladder, so he could climb inside.

When the mud had dried, with his ladder on the wall,
He did not go unnoticed, now being watched by all.
He grabbed his deer skin bed and then he climbed inside,
Safe from desert dangers, he lays upon his hide.

He hears the others talking, he gently cracks a smile,
While others carried water, in pots mile after mile.
The rooms they grew in numbers, everyone built their own,
He was very pleased, with the seed that he had sown.

The word it quickly spread, to others across the sand,
About a distant dreamer, who lived within their land.
For centuries they would build, their homes made from clay,
Because of one great vision, a Navajo had one day.

So, if you have a vision, or you have a distant dream,
And others look down on you and treat you kind of mean.
Remember that one Navajo, out in the desert sand,
Chase your dreams and visions and show your fellow man.

Souls Window

Through the window of my soul, a dream goes drifting by,
I raise the pane to grasp for it, while it's on the fly.
While hanging from soul's window, I grab it with both hands,
I'll fly where it shall take me, off to dreamers' land.

I ride a dream of dreamers, past valleys in my mind,
Over the highest mountains, not measured by the time.
Please open up your window, your soul it has the means,
Release your inner self and fly off with your dreams.

Spring Bouquet

Snow rests on a daffodil, its yellow bright and bold,
Fighting for the season, in midst of springtime cold.
Waiting for that moment, to let its colors shine,
Soon it will become, a daffodil of mine.

I walk into a meadow, with yellow all around,
One by one I pick them, from snow upon the ground.
Then I see a daffodil, just standing all alone,
This one I must have, to take back to my home.

The daffodils I gather, I clamp them in my hand,
Bright and bold they shimmer; springtime is so grand.
I head back to my cabin, to a vase I've chose for them,
When They're placed inside, I'll step back with a grin.

In the center of my table, for everyone to see,
My spring bouquet of daffodils, shining majestically.
Every time I pass them, all throughout the day,
I'll smile upon the daffodils, my newfound spring bouquet.

Ravage Time

You zip on by at ravage pace,
While wrinkles grow upon my face,
You worry not, nor do you care,
Thinning loss, of my Grey hair.

Joints now ache, with slowly gait,
You just watch, and patiently wait.
Like a vulture on a dead branch high,
Waiting for my, spirit to fly.

I notice you high, upon your tree,
Your feathers too, are Grey like me.
But hear the words, roll off my tongue,
Within my heart, I am still young.

So, fly away, go far from here,
I'm not ready, for you so near.
I'll live my life, as young folks do,
No worry of time, no worry of you.

For I'm not one, to sit around,
And wait on you and wear a frown.
I know that someday, we'll meet again,
Until then just fly, upon the wind.

Listen close, my words of rhyme,
You too are stalked, by ravage time.
Don't sit down, try not to stop,
Rewind your ticking, inner clock.

Kick up your heels, and have some fun,
For if you live, you've already won.

Spiritual Friends

I took some time to sit alone, just the other day,
To listen to the spirits and what they had to say.
You can also hear them, and I strongly encourage you do,
I know that you'll be amazed when the spirits speak to you.

I sat upon a mesa's edge, a river far below,
The sky was blue, the sun was high, a wind began to blow.
As the spirits came to me, the breeze it brushed my face,
My eyes were closed, hands in my lap, I was in my spiritual place.

I was visited by the spirit, of a long past Indian chief,
He tells me of a springtime day, he stood in disbelief.
While standing on that Mesa's edge, many years ago,
He seen a hundred Spaniards, on their horses down below.

He tells me of the sparkle, reflecting from their silver Spurs,
He knew someday the sparkle, would try to take his furs.
I could feel the worry in his voice, as his spirit spoke to me,
Then he left just as he came, on a soft and gentle breeze.

Then another spirit came, to speak to me that day,
A woman tells me how she made, many pots of clay.
And how they slowly cured, hard in the desert sun,
Designs that she would paint on them, were loved by everyone.

She said she also took the pots, to tribes that lived nearby,
And traded them for other things, that much improved their lives.
Then just like with the chief, she was there, then gone again,
With no goodbye, she blew away, carried by the wind.

My time upon the Mesa, it seemed to fly by fast,
But I enjoyed the time I spent, with the spirits of the past.
But really, they're more than spirits, carried in the wind,
To me they will always be, my long-lost spirit friends.

Randy's Advice

Remember a fellow searcher, Randy Bilyeu he was called,
He Floated down the Rio Grande, his companion was his dog.
Living out his dreams, looking for a hidden treasure,
He'd be here today if he took more safety measures.

A year has passed since Randy, made his fatal choice,
Now we need to listen and hear his distant voice.
Speaking to all searchers, saying think before you go,
Searching hidden fortunes, traipsing through the snow.

Springs around the corner, wait for it my friend,
Don't become a searcher, that's missing once again.
Indulgence will be waiting, for you to come along,
Warming rays of sunshine, birds will sing their song.

Yes, Randy he has left us, but I know he's very near,
Whispering words to each of us, just listen and you'll here.
Be safe out there my friends, while on your golden quest,
Always be prepared, and I'm wishing you the best.

While chasing all your dreams, whatever you may seek,
Just remember Randy, and a year ago this week.
My fire is warm and cozy, I'm not going out in ice,
I listened to you Randy, thanks for your advice.

My Friends

The chase has got me thinking, about beginnings and the ends,
But most of all I'm thinking, about all my online friends.
Some I've met in person and some I've never met,
Some just met in passing and some I'll never forget.

Jdiggins I want to thank you, you pushed me from the start,
Spallies you are special, you have the biggest heart.
Pdenver your so kind, you're sure an honest friend,
Iron Will you are the bomb, your pies sure make me grin.

Nearindianajones and Keri, nice new friends of mine,
Desertphile I'm still searching, for words to make you shine.
Strawshadow you too inspire me, your words they bring on thought,
Dal your just as awesome, as the blog that you have got.

Anna you're a caring friend, when others are in need,
Mindy nice to meet you, my friend at Fennboree.
Seattlesullivan I must say, your research it is grand,
Ken from down in Georgia, my friend you are the man.

Cynthia,Tom and Jenny, you guys make me grin,
JC1117 I want to thank you, time and time again.
Amy sweitzer with your smiles, you brighten up my day,
Monika up in Canada, my friend from miles away.

Old drum with your stories, keep telling them my friend,
Brooke you'll be my friend, until my very end.
FredY and Doug my buddies, nice as they can be,
I surely can't forget, my friend call MichaelD.

Anthony and Tom terrific, you guys are so neat,
Ramona my friend to me, you're very, very, sweet.
Jimbo and his son, Alex is his name,
Newfound friends of mine, I thank you just the same.

JDA your full of kindness, with soft and gentle words,
And Sparrow you're a friend of mine, soaring like the birds.
Specialklr you my buddy, forever your my friend,
Thank you, amp, for your kindness time again.

I could keep on going, my list goes on and on,
Of friends I'll have until, the day I'm dead and gone.
To those that I've not mentioned, you know just who you are,
Your just as much my friends, your like my shooting stars.

There's one I want to mention, to me a dear true friend,
He set me on adventures, his name is Forrest Fenn.
The chase that he has given, I'll chase it to the end,
But I wouldn't trade a box of gold, for all my online friends.

Never Alone

I sail upon an ocean wide, into the rising sun,
Lost at sea and worried, my day has just begun.
Sailing into the vastness, with my conscious as my friend,
Hoping to spot some land somewhere, before this day has end.

No matter what the outcome, if on this sea I die,
Then I've given it my all, I gave an honest try.
Searching I continued, for any speck of land,
Eating my last bit of food, I held within my hand.

I know I'm sailing fast, there's wind within my sail,
But in this vast and open place, I move just like a snail.
My thirst is getting stronger, as the hours slowly pass,
I try to think some happy thoughts, like water in my glass.

The day drags on, the sun is hot, still listening to my soul,
The wind dies down, the sail it hangs, right beside the pole.
I crawl up to the pointed bow, and kneel upon my knees,
I say a prayer to God above," please help me off this sea ".

I raised up to my feet, and finished with my prayer,
The hanging sail began to rise, filling up with air.
The wind it blew much stronger, than it ever has before,
And pushed me towards, what looks to me, like a busy shore.

The shore it got much closer, as every second passed,
Soon I know I'll have some water, within my empty glass.
When I reached the open beach, with footprints in the sand,
Out I jumped, kissed the ground, so proud to be on land.

I knelt upon the sandy beach, I gazed into the sun,
" Thank you, God, for listening", "now I owe you one".
" I will repay the gift of life", "that you have given me",
"I promise you to tell the story when"," we were lost at sea".

Note from Dad

Wherever your life may take you,
You will always be daddy's girl.
Go and cherish all you do,
I know you'll give it a whirl.

Will you for me, just take the time,
Be faithful in your heart?
There so much here, in heaven's shine,
With me among the stars.

You will miss me, as I miss you,
Stephanie, you are so Great.
I'd love to hug you, once again,
I'll wait at heaven's gate.

Into the Light

Who goes there? Covered by the night,
"Show yourself" I say, and step into the light.
Behind the dark of shadows, a coward place to hide,
"Be brave and come" I say, "stand here at my side".

I gaze into the darkness, a glimpse within the night,
To see a shadow image, approaching to the light.
My thoughts they run astray, I bravely stand my ground,
The calm of night is silent, no eerie little sounds.

Into the light it enters, now just as brave as I,
To my knees I fall, a tear swells in my eye.
Standing there before me, such a peaceful sight,
An angel with her halo, my angel of the night.

Sent from above to guard me, from evil lurking near,
Her voice was softly spoken and soothing to my ears.
She says her job is over, the danger it had passed,
Then flew off in the darkness, came and left so fast.

My angel brought a comfort, there in the black of night,
She bravely came to see me, she stepped into the light.
Whatever's in the darkness, whatever sounds I hear,
I'm not the least bit worried, I know my angel's near.

Look and Listen

The search is ever endless,
Past rivers deep and wide.
Is long ago within us,
Alive down deep inside?

Take a day and set aside,
Time to go explore.
To find what out there surly lies,
Look and look some more.

And tune your ears into the wind,
Listen for their whispered word.
For if you do this, trust me friend,
It is amazing what is heard.

Indian Spirits

Alone I walked into the desert, and sat upon a rise,
Nothing for miles around me, then closed my watering eyes.
I listened close to words not said, that's carried in the wind,
Spirits of the desert Indian, who called this home back then.

The breeze is soft and gentle, and my breathing very slow,
I'm visited by an Indian boy, who lived so long ago.
He tells me of the name he had, they called him Running Bird.
Through his spirit I listened, while clinging to every word.

The desert it was dry and harsh, in Running Birds daily life,
He gathered wood, for the fires, and practiced with his knife.
Knowing someday, a brave he'd be, an honor of every man,
He wanted to be the bravest brave, that ever walked this land.

The sun is setting lower, and a young girl voice I hear,
The wind has brought her here to me, she whispers in my ear.
She says her name is Yellow Cloud, Born at the setting sun,
She helps her mom prepare the meals, enjoyed by everyone.

Knowing someday a wife she'd be, she wanted to be prepared.
She also wore two eagle feathers, tied in her long black hair.
The tribe was very happy, everyone played their part,
The spirit of the desert Indian lived deep within their hearts.

Next, I heard an old man's voice, also carried in the wind,
He said he was a mighty chief, for that desert tribe back then.
He told me of a special day, many, many years ago,
They shouted, sang and danced, before the winter snows.

Because of two young Indians, all chants they could be heard.
The joining hearts of Yellow Cloud, and her young brave Running Bird.
The sun is setting low, and the wind is dying down,
Time for me to leave this place, and head back into town.

Before I leave, I raise my hands, say bye to Running Bird,
Yellow Cloud and the mighty Chief and thanked them for their words.
Next time you're in the desert, and your walking all alone,
Take the time, listen to spirits, of the Indians who called this home.

Pow Wow

Would you please take the time, just picture what I say?
The sky above is blue, it's a nice and sunny day.
People gather in numbers, in their native gear,
A Pow Wow for the Navajo, festivities for the year.

Many wore their headdresses, feathers to the ground,
Children's painted faces, drums heard all around.
With breast beads on their front, moccasins on their feet,
Every color of the rainbow, such a sight to see.

Some were dressed as birds, they danced with open wings,
Others played their flutes, while the sounds of spirits sing.
Hides were stretched across, handmade native drums,
Painted with bright colors, admired by everyone.

When they struck the hide, with their hand-held sticks,
The boom it sounds like thunder, with every solid lick.
Some arrived on horses, which too were painted bright,
With beads tied in the mane, I'll never forget the sight.

I noticed how the little ones, barely three feet tall,
Were also in their native dress, showing off for all.
Fires were burning near, the smoke was rising high,
Leaving clouds of Grey, against the pale blue sky.

Everyone was mingling, with their native friends,
Enjoying their time of fellowship, everyone wore a grin.
When the day was over, the crowd it drifts away,
The sound of drums they faded, sun setting on this day.

I think the world should stop and learn from native friends,
This world sure needs a Pow Wow, it'll help it in the end.

Simple Treasures

Alone within a mountain tent,
Lying on my sleeping bag.
Thinking of the day I've spent,
The adventures that I've had.

The forest it is talking,
Beyond my nylon wall.
Small critters gently walking,
A lonesome hoot owl call.

The wind is softly blowing,
Tree shadows on my tent.
In thought my mind keeps going,
To the places that I've went.

Stars fill the nighttime sky,
Beyond the net above.
Life is very grand for me,
Just doing what I love.

I'm looking for a treasure,
Here in these mountains wide.
No words can even measure,
To what I feel inside.

And if I never find it,
Then that's ok by me.
I know the treasure sits,
Outside surrounding me.

In peace I drift away,
Into a silent slumber.
With thoughts of one great day,
Below this mountain sky I'm under.

For me I have no sorrow,
Moon shines upon the trees.
I dream of my tomorrow,
And what treasures it will bring.

Pauley T

If you were a fool and found you some gold,
Yep, you'd fool me, with the gold that you found.
But if you found me, with a fool and your gold,

Together this fool, would help with your mound.
So, don't fool yourself if you find you some gold,
This fool would help carry, the gold that you found.

Small Deeds

The morning's still,
The dew it rests.
Upon a blade of grass,
I find the will.

Hands on my chest,
Reflecting the past.
Upon your stone,
Etched in black.

A time so long ago,
Though you are gone.
Not coming back,
Your memory still it flows.

Beside your stone,
Some flowers pink.
Cracking morning rays,
You may be gone.

I often think,
About joining you someday.
The time I took,
A little while.

Goodbye I softly say,
One last look.
Crack a smile,
Then I walk away.

Trail of Dreams

What once was shiny, bright and bold,
Now dims by time, the trail runs cold.
Imagination, throughout the wood,
Then yet again, there time stood.

Probing, prodding, my every move,
As if I have, so much to prove.
Dreams of old, that once were new,
Fade like a summer, morning dew.

Though I get tired, Time never rests,
It wants to prove, that it's the best.
I know someday, it will prevail,
I'll lose the wind, within my sail.

Until my winds, no longer blow,
I'll fight like hell, before I go.
So, go now Time, use all your means,
We'll meet again, on my trail of dreams.

The Trail of Tears 1838-39

Upon a mountain trail I walked, I left my car behind,
Not caring where I went, not knowing what I'd find.
For hours I walked along this trail, my mind it drifts away,
To another distant time, of a forgotten distant day.

I stopped upon the lonely trail and then removed my boots,
So, I could feel the history, bare feet of Cherokee roots.
Many walked this very trail, carrying food in bowls,
Babies on their back, pride deep within their souls.

I take the time to pause and smell of the aromas,
Smelt also by the Cherokee, on their way to Oklahoma.
Some elders couldn't make it, too weak to walk this path,
Months of walking westward, after a bloody wrath.

Many fell upon this trail, never to rise again,
They left this trail in spirit, carried in the wind.
.
Those who sadly finished, had tears within their eyes,
Placed on a reservation, but not to their surprise.

Up ahead I see a rock, to rest my aching feet,
They too have sat upon that rock, heads hung in defeat.
History isn't always, as pleasant as can be,
But it's history none the less, here for you and me.

I hope that we have learned, from our history way back then,
Never again to cause, more spirits in the wind.
It's time for me to turn around, back to the truck I'll go,
The air is getting cooler, the sun is getting low.

If I could say one thing, to all your listening ears,
Never forget the Cherokee and their swollen eyes with tears.

The Ride

Winds of time blow,
Onward we go.
Riding the wind,
Reins in hands.

Over great lands,
Beginning to end.
Be not judged,
Hold no grudge.

Love for all,
Upon your ride.
No secrets hide,
Your reins will fall.

Lead by hands,
Of other lands.
Shepherds of the light.
Dismount my friend.

To walk within,
A place so ever bright.

True Peace

You'll gaze into the heavens, in deepest thought alone,
And never will you doubt, where those before have gone.
There you'll find serenity, a warm and loving touch,
A kind of peace and freedom, you've never felt so much.

Your hearts a product of, a loving higher hand,
Pumping peace and love, your mind will understand.
Live from in your heart, until your final day,
Then others they'll see you, as fears are cast away.

They'll stop and listen closely, to peaceful words you say,
Take time to share with others, your message day to day.
Give your peace to others, share what's true and sound,
Heart to heart, friend to friend, embrace the peace you've found.

The Stand Off

Warriors of a noble tribe, upon their horses sat,
Side by side all in a line, the day was cold and wet.
They gazed across a meadow, as blue coats sat the same,
Painted and in silence and not a chant was sang.

The minutes slowly passed, with strong and ready stares,
Spears within their hands and feathers from their hair.
With faces painted boldly, on horses painted too,
Awaiting on the blue coats, to make a deadly move.

Within the midst of silence, with tension all around,
A warrior he dismounts and stands upon the ground.
With his spear in hand, he paces towards the coats,
All dressed for the battle, a claw hung from his throat.

He split the distance bravely, his spear held in his hand,
Quickly he then stuck it, into their precious land.
He walked back and remounted and gave a steady eye,
No weapon for the battle, no fear for if he dies.

The leader of the blue coats, with stripes upon his sleeve,
He rode out to the spear, so that all awaiting sees.
And with his rifle high, he nodded to the brave,
It's not a day for battle, then they rode their separate ways.

Upon the Sand

Feel the gentle sandy beads,
The caressing, soothing hand.
Warmth upon your tiresome feet,
As you stroll across the sand.

You just self-reflecting,
Walk with a gaze up high.
Casually remembering,
Through years that passed on by.

The footprints on your endeavor,
Sands art from which you stand.
Of course, now framed forever,
Time spent upon the sand.

The Rio Grande

In the spring of 1540, along the Rio Grande,
The Navajo lived in peace and harmony with the land.
The reason that I know this, a spirit told me so,
While sitting near the water edge, many years ago.

The spirits name was" Running Bird ", he lived there long ago,
He began his planting, just after the melting snows.
One day while he was planting, the sun was very high,
Then high upon a Mesa top, something caught his eye.

He stopped what he was doing and stared up at the top,
The men were all on horseback, it looked as if they stopped.
He just stood there looking and totally amazed,
The flicker from their silver, dancing in the Rays.

He ran back to the pueblo, while warning every man,
Strangers are among us, strangers in our lands.
It was some Spanish riders, with silver on their Spurs,
The Navajo braced themselves, for whatever did occur.

They rode down from the Mesa top, picking up their pace,
The Navajo grabbed their spears, ready to defend their place.
The Spaniards rode into the village, Running Bird called his home,
Then some shots were fired and then a spear was thrown.

It didn't take them very long, the Navajo they gave in,
They knew they couldn't match, the arms of Spanish men,
For years, the Spanish lived there, controlling how they'd live,
Running Bird couldn't stand it, all he did was give.

One night while Spanish slept, some elders gathered round,
And talked about how they could, regain their sacred ground.
Running Bird, he was chosen, to do a mighty task,
Very proud and honored, he done just what they ask.

He took some tiny ropes, with knots tied in a line,
He'd run them to all pueblos, to tell them when the time.
Each day a knot removed, until the final knot,
Then they would rise up and give the Spanish all they got.

When that day arrived, every Navajo man,
Fought and ran the Spaniards, completely from their lands.
Again, they lived in harmony, for many years to come,
But watched upon the Mesa tops, for Spaniards with their guns.

Sometimes you got to stand up, for things you know are right,
Fill your rope with knots, get ready for your fight.
Running Bird, he's a hero, for uniting every man,
I was honored to hear his spirit, sitting by the Rio Grande.

Where I Sit

No time in thought is wasted,
One there can travel far.
Can my thoughts alone,
Think past a distant star?

My answer to my question,
Thoughts have no earthly bound.
The dreams that lie within me,
Journey far past mother's ground.

Is this your day to journey?
Only you can make the trip.
Mine will be a great one,
Alone here where I sit.

Lessons Learned

Lessons learned, though wounds were deep, glazed by scars,
Lessons learned, though eyes do weep, neath distant stars.
Lessons learned, though heart does break, leaking tears within,
Lessons learned, though torn apart, ripped by ravage sin.

Lessons learned, though stepped upon, by feet of enemy,
Lessons learned, though dagger pierced, into the side of thee.
Lessons learned, though bleeding heart, emptying your soul,
Lessons learned, though tears were caught, in overflowing bowl.

Wisdom is sometimes painful, many years you yearned,
But God will stand beside you, while though your lessons learned.

Life's Journey

The journey of mankind,
Real through living eyes.
Voyage through given time,
Of ultimate surprise.

Discovery that awaits,
Consists of many wails.
Not locked behind life's gate,
In forbidden weary tales.

Seeking journeys bold,
New within your grasp.
Lands still yet untold,
But holding secrets past.

Seeing through life's venue,
With wide and open gaze.
New journeys will await you,
Eyes twinkle with amaze.

Knowledge

He was the sacred bird of Thoth, with scepter in his hand,
The balance of the universe, mighty umpire of the land.
Neither good nor bad could take control, though both sides they have tried,
Thoth, he kept them both in check, and never missed a stride.

Egyptian wall of pictures, now tell us of their myths,
In Thoth's new form of writing, we know as hieroglyphs.
For at least a couple thousand years, they've wrote upon their walls,
Boldly in the passages, of their long and narrow halls.

Through their writings we have learned that gold it has a power,
Owned mostly by Egyptian kings, who lived in that ancient hour.
Gold it was the skin of Gods, priceless to all kings,
But wisdom held the greatest power, way above all things.

Because of Thoth the God of Wisdom, knowledge spread the lands,
Then they lived a better life, across those arid sands.
Homes they built with massive stones, pointed at the top,
Wisdom helped them manage those, huge and massive rocks.

I believe there is a lesson here, in the lives of ancient kings,
It's not about the gold we have, or our bright shiny things.
It's more about our knowledge, that we pass on down the line,
So, generations after us, can also live as fine.

We too can write upon our wall, for a thousand years ahead,
The future will then know of us, and the knowledge that we had.
Pass your wisdom on to others, so they can also strive,
To live a life of knowledge, and in death they'll feel alive.

Lock & Key

Contentment is the lock,
Imagination is the key.
When both they come together,
Oh, glorious sights you'll see.

Monday

If you were on your way to yesterday,
You must have left today.
Tuesday seems too far away,
Possibly it was Monday?

Strange things happen on that day,
Because the weekend seems so far away.
If I had to guess a single day,
It's Monday I would say.

What? What is today?
Monday!
Be careful my friend in work or play,
Strange things happen on days like today.

Legends

Just sitting here reflecting, to legends no longer here,
With Beethoven's Moonlight Sonata, playing to my ears.
Thinking about the brush strokes and Mona Lisa's smile,
By Leonardo Da Vinci, who's been a legend for a while.

Many great poets dipped their quill, in ink wells years ago,
To create masterpieces like The Raven, by Edgar Allen Poe.
Thought provoking words, we've loved throughout the years,
Mere players upon a worldly stage, written by William Shakespeare.

Many poets shared their work, since they first began,
But Emily Dickinson, in her closet, hid most all of them.
I could keep on going, about poets and their ways,
And how they took their thoughts and wrote them on a page.

There was also legend Chiefs, that walked upon this land,
Geronimo and Crazy Horse, were two that walked back then.
Like Sitting Bull they wanted peace, to rest upon their people,
Not forced away to distant lands and forced in Spanish steeples.

George Washington, our founding father, came over on a boat,
With visions for a better place, that we can call our home.
There are legends all around us, that made their mark back then,
Thank you for your visions, you're a Legend Forrest Fenn.

California Gold Rush 1848

In the year of 1848, out in the Cali sand,
He lived and worked with pride, a kind and gentle man.
James Marshall was a foreman, the leader of his crew,
One day about mid-morning, the sky above was blue.

With their picks and shovels, down in their hand dug ditch,
James he noticed something, that soon would make him rich.
At his feet there laid, a nugget made of gold,
For days he kept his secret, not a single soul was told.

Then one day while walking, with a longtime friend,
He told him what he had found, news traveled like the wind.
As it quickly traveled, "there's gold out in the west",
Many grabbed their pans, to put them to the test.

With hopes and dreams they traveled, their wagons in a line,
They came in by the thousands, in search of better times.
Some they dug in holes, many others lined the creeks,
Panning for their fortune, for many, many weeks.

The weeks turned into months, the months turned into years,
Some they found their gold, many others left in tears.
The gold rush slowly faded, empty shacks were left behind,
Tracks that guided cars, stretched from every mine.

James he stayed behind, to live a happy life,
Just rocking on his porch, beside him rocked his wife.
For years reporters asked, for years his stories told,
But now between them sits, their heavy sack of gold.

Canadian Sunrise

The morning light is here, the sun has yet to rise,
I see a flock of geese, against the morning sky.
A lake I have before me, a dock extending out,
This to me is living, what life is all about.

I stroll on out the dock and sit down at the end,
I think about my life, how great that it has been.
Looking to the east, the sun begins to rise,
Reflecting off the water, into my morning eyes.

Then I hear a splash, it breaks my silent morn,
Fish begin their feeding; I'm tossing in some corn.
They come in by the numbers, a breakfast treat for them,
Until my can is empty, I feed them with a grin.

I raise up to my feet and turn to walk away,
While walking on the dock, I hear a voice just say.
"I'll always be here for you, whenever you're in need",
I turn and look behind me, nothing there but me.

I feel a subtle warmness, in chilly morning air,
I knew my God was with me, I know he truly cares.
I take a final look, with peace within my eyes,
Nothing beats my mornings, my Canadian sunrise.

Chimayo Dirt

Here I sit within my chair, my legs don't work to well,
Even if I rub them, they hurt and sometimes swell.
A friend once had told me, of a place out in the west,
Legends say it's special, puts miracles to the test.

In a town they call Chimayo, there sits a little church,
Nestled by the river, where miracles grow in bursts.
Guided by our God, for whom we love so much,
Dirt within a back room, has his healing touch.

I pack my bags for travel, this place now I must go,
Really, I want to feel, his miracle in my toes.
Tired of my two legs, just lifeless laying there,
Out the door I roll, my ride is finally here,

Friends like this is special, he knows I feel it's right,
Cross the country we travel, the town is now in sight,
Here awaits a miracle, the church he rolls me in,
I can't believe my eyes; all I can do is grin.

Many pics and stories, of miracles one by one,
And with a fist of dirt, my miracle has just begun.
Yes, that is when I stood, my legs no longer hurt,
Oh "thank you God" I praised, for his miracle in that dirt.

Fly Away

We seek for gold, a treasures lore,
But shall we seek, for so much more?
The sparkle of, a diamonds shine,
Cannot shine past, the end of time.

Nor massive nuggets, of earthly weight,
Bare the same, at our futures gate.
So, as I gaze, into my fire,
I search for answers, my heart's desire.

An emeralds green, a sapphires blue,
Will stay behind, once I am through.
My mind like flames, it dances around,
To realize my treasure, I've already found.

My peace within, my internal gold,
It's weight I bare, my heart it holds.
So, if today's, my final day,
I'll take my treasures, and I'll fly away.

Freedom's Honor

Proudly I fly, as my colors I wave,
To remind our great mighty, home of brave.
In the dark of night, so brightly I'll stand,
For all the freedoms, of our fellow man.

My colors I'll show, so proudly I'll bear,
Forever I'll shine, up in the night air.
My colors won't run, back down to a crawl,
For your freedom I'll fly, for each of you all.

For those who defend, for the freedoms of me,
In the wave of my colors, your bravery we see.
For those who have died, now home and at rest,
Freedom thanks you with honor, as I lay on your chest.

A Knicker in The Night

Many, many years ago, in scorching summer sand,
A Navajo man awaits, for nightfall in his land.
Within a narrow cactus shade, the only one for miles,
Though thirsty, hot and weathered, he cracks a gentle smile.

Deep within his thoughts, fond memories he recalls,
Like days that he spent soaking, beneath the mountain falls.
And hunting through the winter, in snowflakes cold and white.
And resting on the Mesa top, while eagles soar in flight.

His horse has spooked and left him, there in this arid space,
The paint below his sweating brow, runs down his weary face.
Then as the sun was setting, he leaves his shaded perch,
While gazing for his horse, he resumes his needed search.

For hours he slowly walked, while always looking down,
In search of one lost horse track, imbedded in the ground.
His luck then quickly changes, he finds his horses trail,
Thinking of the story, that someday he could tell.

Calling in the moonlight, he feels his horse is near,
Praying that his voice, will catch his horse's ear.
Then near a desert boulder, his horse comes into sight,
As he hears a friendly sound, of a knicker in the night.

A Flags Honor

Proudly I fly, as my colors I wave,
To remind our great mighty, home of the brave.
In the dark of the night, so brightly I'll stand,
For all the freedoms, of our fellow man.

My colors I'll show, so proudly I'll bear,
Forever I'll shine, up in the night air.
My colors won't run, back down to a crawl,
In your memory I'll fly, for each of you all.

For those who defend, for the freedoms of me,
In the wave of my colors, your bravery we see.
For those who have died, now home and at rest,
In honor I thank you, as I lay on your chest.

4rest4fend

It's not the rhythm, nor the rhyming,
Not the wisdom, or even chiming.
The wonders in, composed sensation,
Halts a beavers, true imagination.

Blank Slate

I came into this world so frail, blank slate in which to write,
Loved ones wrote the first few words, with caring chalk of white.
Words were small and simple, my mind was very young,
From that moment forward, my eager mind begun.

Beside my growing mind of slate, an eraser you would find,
To remove unwanted words of Grey, not needed in my mind.
Decade past my slate has grown, my mind is taking shape,
Nourished by the ones who care, still writing on my slate.

Word by word, my list grew long, with each passing year,
Speaking words of wisdom, to those who want to hear.
Many, many years have passed, my hair is turning Grey,
On my slate a million words since that fragile day.

Now sitting in a waiting room, for my grandchild I do wait.
To come into this world so frail and with an empty slate.
Simple words I've chosen and with my chalk in hand,
To write upon an empty slate, that's tender and so grand.

Time has come to write my words, first words to start anew,
Gently with my chalk of white, I write I love you.
Beside my growing grandchild, I will walk throughout the years,
Oh, the stories I will tell, to fill those tender ears.

We all have words of wisdom, written on our slate of time,
Take moment, choose some words and pass them down the line.
Help a growing slate of words, begin a brand-new start,
If you do this, trust in me, you will feel it in your heart.

A Redneck Kind of Christmas

A coon dog on the sofa, it is just too cold outside,
A record in the player, plays "Oh Holy Night".
Christmas lights are strung, around the window at the door,
No need to take them down, left from the year before.

The ceiling fan it wobbles, keeping rhythm with the tune,
Then a holler to the kids, "ya'll Santa's coming soon".
He must use the front door, this trailer has no flue,
Explain that to the young ins, not an easy thing to do.

This redneck country Christmas, by far the best in years,
"Whoever is in the bathtub, you wash behind them ears".
There are cookies in the oven, for Santa's midnight snack,
The energy he needs, to lift that hefty sack.

"Settle down you kids, quit running down the hall",
Then the youngest of the five, sits down and starts to bawl.
I rare back on the sofa, by blue and grab my head.
"I think I hear ole Santa, you kids go jump in bed".

But really, I heard nothing, I need a tiny break,
A little peace and quiet, not much for goodness sake.
Then poof the kids were gone, ran down the narrow hall,
I forgot about the cookies, by Gosh I burnt them all.

I tossed them out the back door, the kids they'll never know,
That is when I noticed, a light but falling snow.
Asleep the kids are silent, me and momma by ole blue,
Arm in arm we rest, with nothing left to do.

Early in the morning, before the morning sun,
I will hear their tiny feet, running one by one.
I would not trade our Christmas, best day throughout the year,
To see their smiling faces, with ole blue just resting near.

Bluebirds Serenade

Upon a gentle mountain breeze, a bluebird sails along,
Looking for a place to perch, to sing his lovely song.
Over the hidden treetops, covered with light snow,
He passes by a window, the window to my soul.

He sees my windows open, he gently flies within,
To land upon my branches, to sing his lovely hymn.
I listen to the music, a bluebird's serenade,
That Echoes through my soul, while playing on my stage.

When his song was over and he took to flight again,
Leaving me with memories, of a bluebird's heavenly hymn.
Back through the window of my soul, the bluebird he retreats,
Back into the mountains, to float upon the breeze.

My Windows always open, for birds that come along,
So, they can perch and rest, to chirp their favorite song.
There are little things among us, don't miss them as you go,
Go and open your window, the window to your soul.

Then as a bluebird's passing and sees your windows high,
Maybe he will stop and sing for you, as he's passing by.
You'll enjoy his music, a bluebird's melody.
I know because I've heard it, he stopped and sang for me.

An Eagles Cry

We gaze across the valley, they are mounted side by side,
Strangers in our homeland, we will not run and hide.
Upon our painted ponies, we bravely sit the same,
Waiting for the moment, we hear their first shot ring.

We are at a disadvantage, the morning sun is low,
Rising back behind them, in our eyes the morning glowed.
The tension it was rising, no sounds are heard at all,
Then suddenly it was broken, a screech, an eagle's call.

A message from the heavens, great spirit in the sky,
"Fight for your Native lands, for freedom proudly die".
Behind our painted ponies, our homes of tanned deer hides,
We hear a newborn baby, her precious little cry.

We hear their trumpet blow, all rifles raised at us,
Behind the stranger's ponies, clouds of valley dust.
We too take off like lightning, into the valley wide,
Chanting on our ponies, we will reach the other side.

We met down in the valley, their shots like thunder rang,
Our battle it was here, our arrows flew the same.
The strangers fell in numbers, with arrows in their breast,
We too had warriors fall, with holes within their chest.

The battle briefly lasted, the strangers turned and run,
Back into the glow, of the early morning sun.
We rode back to our village and as we rode inside,
Some women they were happy, while others knelt and cried.

This morning we were tested, we bravely stood our ground,
Some warriors left in spirit, while others stayed around.
I gazed off in the valley, I ask the reason, why?
Again, the mighty spirit, answered with an eagle's cry.

168 *James Bynum*

Bedtime Hero

Through the door of darkness shines, a light to show the way,
The beams emit before me, turning black to Grey.
A single step before me, I know that I must take,
Across this blackened threshold, afraid and wide awake.

I feel that there are things that hide, in the darkness I can't see,
With illuminating eyes, that are focused right on me.
The world is in some trouble, on me it now depends,
I'll go into the darkness, no matter how it ends.

I hear the thunders rumble, like feet upon the stairs,
With a dash I entered, to save the world who cares.
The thunder it gets closer, I cover up my head,
That's when Mom just spoke to me, she saw me jump in bed.

Her words were soft and gentle, in moms own caring way,
I'll save the world another time, within the light of day.
Then she took my sword, and my favorite batman cape,
Tucked me in and left me, in my darkened little space.

Now I lay me down to sleep, I say all to myself,
With my flashlight shining at, my sword upon the shelf.
Morning when I wake, I will fight the villains who's mean,
While planning how I would do it, I drift into my dreams.

A Haiku for Castaway

Go breath the night air,
Crisp and cool in the mountains,
Exhale your worries.

The Scout

In the year of 1860, I was riding on my horse,
Scouting for the Navajo, trying to plot a course.
I ride up to the Mesa top, where I can see the land,
Walk over to the edge, I can see the desert span.

Way off in the distant, there's rising campfire smoke,
Looks like a camp of white men, all wearing dark blue coats.
They've brought with them their rifles, also their bloody wrath,
I must go back and warn them and change our dangerous path.

As I ride up to my tribe, the chief he welcomes me,
I tell him of the camp ahead and everything I've seen.
Now it's up to him, the leader of us all,
The choice now he must make, for the safety of us all.

Our chief begins to speak, while sitting on his horse,
He says we'll ride into the sun, and slightly change our course.
Again, I take off riding, the sun glaring in my eyes,
Slowly they ride behind me, hoping for no surprise.

I ride along the river, until the sun is low,
No sign of the invaders, wearing their blue coats.
When I reached the mountains, the rivers crystal clear,
I find a lush green meadow, and in it several deer.

I turn and ride back to my tribe and say it's safe and sound,
This time I tell our chief, about the meadow I have found.
The women they are tired, with children on their backs,
The men were slumping over, with belongings in their sacks.

The chief he raised his hand, every ear was tuned,
He says our journeys short now, ending very soon.
He looks at me and says, "now lead us to that place",
Upon my paint I ride, a smile upon my face.

When we reached the meadow, the chief he raised his voice,
In his weathered face, you could see he made his choice.
He says" the waters clear, even though the deer had gone,
Welcome to our meadow, welcome to your home".

Tiny Flames

Smoke is rising, embers falling, into the nighttime air,
Alone beside her campfire, a Navajo woman stares.
Lost within the coals of red, her mind it drifts away,
Thinking of the many years, now many moons away.

Wrinkles upon her aging face, her hair a silver glaze,
In thought just reminiscing, of bright and younger days.
She remembers to a time, her eldest child was born,
Amidst a strong and violent, springtime thunderstorm.

But now he is a man, so many years have passed,
She wondered how that time, could move so very fast.
She looked up to the heavens and pondered reasons why,
Above her stars like diamonds, filled the nighttime sky.

As the fire slowly fades, a bed of coals remains,
She pokes while staring at them, the dancing tiny flames.
To her the answers simple, she knew it from the start,
It's not about the years you live, it's how you live within your heart.

Tribute to MLK

A determined voice heard, upon this day,
Speaks unity amongst, a world in dismay.
Equality was short, in our states united,
Words rang out, across a country divided.

In search of dreams, as all living should,
To end the ashes, where crosses once stood.
Through lurking evils, determined moves on,
Not vowing to stop, till his words were all gone.

A nation then listened, to the ring of his voice,
The color of skin's, not anyone's choice.
The blood is still red, no matter the race,
United a country, put it back in its place.

The flag is our symbol, stars with great bands,
Defending it proudly, United we stand.
Together we'll rise, through visions once seen,
Because we're a country, who lives out our dreams.

James Bynum

Little Fellow

I too have seen that little fellow,
With colors bright and bold.
Reds and greens with brightest yellows,
Oh, what secrets does he hold?

Moonlit Drums

In the year of 1540, near a mountain meadows side,
A grazing deer just stops and holds his head up high.
He sees the other deer, they quickly turn and run,
In the glowing moonlight, he hears a distant drum.

The deer it slowly paces, one short step at a time,
Towards the sound of drums, as if he wants to find.
He left the moonlit meadow, guided by his ears,
The sound of drums grew louder, not showing any fear.

Then he reached a bluff line, the deer he had to stop,
Below the fires they flickered, as he stood there on the top.
The sound of drums just rumbled, just below his stance,
Around the fire in circles, the Indians quickly danced.

The deer just stood there staring, amazed at what he saw,
In the sound of native drums, he hears the Indians' call.
Then he sees a shooting star, race across the sky,
As he turns to leave, with reflections in his eyes.

The deer just walks away, back through the aspens dark,
As the natives fire below, into the sky threw sparks.
Then he reached the meadow and grazing once again,
In the sound of moonlit drums, missed by all his friends.

Lifelong Dreams

Through gentle strokes an artist's brush, his vision lay in oils,
Striving for perfections best, no blemishes or spoils.
Upon a wall while spotlight shines, gazed by passerby,
Years they pass, old oil it cracks, still pleasing to the eye.

A bow is pulled, Stradivarius sings, in tones majestically,
Swaying to his music, eyes closed and cannot see.
Alone he plays upon a stage, a thousand empty chairs,
Bent at the waist he takes a bow, as silence fills the air.

Dipped in ink, a writer's quill, upon the paper writes,
A candle burns, his thoughts are written, up into the night.
Page by page a book is formed, the writer lays his pen,
Words now read by millions, best seller from way back then.

If you have a dream my friends, like paint, music and ink,
Feel it, live it and chase it and take some time and think.
Let your talents shine, be the next new biggest thing,
Live life to the fullest, while chasing your lifelong dreams.

Little Old Lady

Christmas season upon me, I went out for a stroll,
To admire all the lights, while they glistened, and they glowed.
The evening was cold, a light snow in the air,
Each house I would stop, on the curb and just stare.

Ahead on the corner, a café is in sight,
Hot chocolate sounds good, to top off this night.
The door was lit up and so was the steps,
But sitting there on them, a lady just wept.

I knelt down beside her, and asked, if she was alright,
Then Removing her hood, oh what a sight.
A little old lady, tears rolled down her face,
Standing there staring, I just froze in my space.

I ask her to join me, and welcomed her in,
I could tell she needed, some words of a friend.
I ordered us chocolate, she was wiping her eyes,
The words that she spoke, caught me by surprise.

"my husband is gone now", "I lost him last week",
" For 55 years", "we strolled down this street".
" Admiring the lights", "stopping here for some tea".
" No family at all", "none now just me".

Speechless I stare, my heartstrings were tugged,
That's when I rose, and I gave her a hug.
While hugging I told her, there's no need to cry,
Cause now I'm her family, till the day that I die.

We left the warm cafe, and continued to walk,
With a Smile on her face, she steadily talked.
I could tell she, needed a friend,
I opened my heart, and welcomed her in.

When our walk in the night, came to an end,
She gave me a hug, said" thank you my friend".
I looked at her, her eyes were still red,
With a Hand on each shoulder, then that's when I said.

" we're now more than friends", "we're family for life",
" Till the day that I die", "I'll be by your side".
The smile on her face, said all it could say,
One final hug, and we parted our ways.

From that day on, each year as they pass,
We'd stroll down that street and stop for a glass.
The family I gained, while I went for a stroll,
Will never again, go weep in the cold.

If your ever out walking, just taking it in,
And you see somebody, just needing a friend.
Please take the time, to tell them you care,
And show them how family will always be there.

Let Me Know

Ever since that dreadful day, out in the desert west,
I've searched for chilly winds, with a warmness in my chest.
I'm looking for my special friend, a spirit of long ago,
She brought me special healing when it was time for me to go.

I know that she was sent to me, from God way up above,
A messenger of heavens mail sealed with a touch of love.
When evil lurked around me and the pain it filled my chest,
That is when my loving faith, was put through a mighty test.

I still recall the dreadful day, that her spirit came to me,
5 years have quickly passed away, but her vision I can see.
A ghostlike faded image, she looked Apache bred,
Maybe in her twenties, with a bandanna around her head.

Holding down her hair of black, silky, long and straight,
With a handmade woven belt, just tied around her waist.
Her deerskin robe it hung, to just about her knees,
Her hair was gently blowing, standing in that chilly breeze.

Her face it had a calming glow, her eyes were filled with love,
Her voice was softly spoken, as if speaking from above.
My spirit friend I miss her, but until we meet again,
I'll stroll across these deserts, in search of chilly winds.

The odds were stacked against me, my end was very near,
Her spirit was sent to save me, so others now can hear.
If your hiking in a desert, then a cool wind starts to blow,
And you see my spirit friend, would you please, just let me know?

Molly

Molly has a purpose, I'm sure you know I'm right,
Sleeping in the day but guarding through the night.
To keep a watchful eye, so you can sleep with ease,
Not wanting in return, she's only there to please.

A friend who walks beside you, not wanting very much,
A ball within the yard, or a gentle petting touch.
Though she speaks no words, her actions say it all,
Always there beside you and at your beacon call.

To look into her eyes, loyalty you will see,
Regardless of her size, shape or even breed.
Friends they come and go, like leaves upon the wind,
Not those like good ole Molly, known as man's best friend.

In Here to Play

Many come to the Poetry Page, to relax or maybe play,
or just to rest their weary minds, from a thoughtful day.
We are all like tiny pieces, of a puzzle not yet done,
even though we are many, together we are one.

Many words are spoke here, some funny, and some sad,
But spoken none the less, to me that makes me glad.
Even though I speak here, I have never written a poem before,
Not until ole Forrest Fenn, opened my door.

We are all but tiny pieces, when matched we are locked in,
To create a mighty masterpiece, to give to Mr. Fenn.
To hang upon his adobe wall, to look at every day,
From friends here at the poetry page, who just came in here to play.

Memories Playground

Memories I've made, in this ultimate chase,
No ravage of time could ever erase.
Etched in my mind, like written on stone,
Anytime I can relive them, while sitting at home.

Sometimes I wonder, if the chase were to end,
Would some folks on this blog, remain to be friends?
Some they would fade, and go on their way,
Never to be heard, in this life that we play.

Other friends that were made, right here in the chase,
Will play their part, with a smile on their face.
If that day, in my lifetime arrives,
Let's meet in Santa Fe and talk about the prize.

Until that day, my memories I'm making,
Looking for a chest, that's there for the taking.
Thank you, Forrest, For the ultimate race,
Because friendships are made in" The Thrill of The Chase".

There's Dal, Goofy and the one Diggin Gypsy.
To many to mention, some who seem tipsy.
Jdiggins and CindyM, on the poetry space,
Let's not forget Amy, with a smile on her face.

Spallies, so kind, and wiseone so smart,
We all want to finish, but first we must start.
To many to mention, I'll be here all day,
So, Let's make some memories, in Forrest's playground we play.

The Bush

Through a bush of burning red,
A father smiles from overhead.
He knows he shapes a subtle grin,
Just waiting till you meet again.

The Bush it stands, new seasons start,
It drops its seeds, to warm your heart.

Story I Can Tell

I have walked along the edge,
I even slipped and fell.
With all my might, I climbed back up,
Oh, the story I can tell.

The Bath

The year was 1640, in what we call Yellowstone,
There lived an Indian boy, he called that place his home.
One day he went out walking, with his spear in hand,
Along a steaming Creek, there in that magical land.

He followed the heated creek, winding through the trees,
Going to his special place, he knew that it would please.
He popped out of the wood line, a river in front of him,
Steam rising in the distant, he gave a subtle grin.

He walked down to the river's edge, where the small creek ends,
Onto the rocks he laid his spear, then slowly waded in.
The water it was warm, it was steaming just a bit,
With his arms spread out, to hold him where he sits.

He laid his head back on a rock and stared up to the sky,
The sky above was blue, he heard an Eagles cry.
Lost within the solitude, of that magical place,
His mind could drift away, to any time in space.

When his dreams have ended, it was time for him to go,
Dripping wet and warm, a steady south wind blows.
With his spear in hand, back up the creek he walked,
His soul had been replenished, bare feet upon the rocks.

He turns around for one last look, steam rising in the sky,
Thankful for this place, you could see it in his eyes.
When he got back home, he sat upon a log,
Relaxed there in his memory, of bathing in the fog.

Spiritual Gifts

Deep within, a forest boundary,
Stands a rock cliff, straight and tall.
Steaming as if, poured in a foundry,
From top of it, warm water falls.

Kneeling upon, its steaming banks,
An Indian brave, with knees in sand.
While in his silence, he gives his thanks,
Into warm water, released from his hands.

Upon a hand carved, boat made of bark,
Two willow leaves of a lone nearby tree.
Three feathers of Grey, from a meadowlark,
One bloody arrowhead, that was pulled from he.

The brave he gently, takes in a deep breath,
Sending his boat, down that river of heat.
He remembers the face, of the angel of death,
While chanting aloud, he then rose to his feet.

Looks at the heavens, then softly he said,
"Two willow leaves", "are the lives that you give".
"Three feathers for angels"," that circled my head",
" One bloody arrowhead", "removed so I live".

"Thank you, great spirit,", "up there in the sky",
" For giving me life"," so proudly I'll stay".
"Great heavens above"," accept all my pride",
Then slowly he turns and just walks away.

Upon the warm River, his boat drifts away,
Quickly it floated, though haven't a sail.
The heavens then answered, heard by the brave,
The silence was broken, by a loud eagles' wail.

A Distant Land

Though I live in a land down under,
I read the poem and often wonder.
And with my toes down in the sand,
I dream about a distant land.

As the ocean slaps the shore,
I dream about his gold galore.
Someday soon, I will cross the span,
I dream about a distant land.

As for now, I will sit right here,
Soak in the sun and drink my beer.
But as my drink turns warm and bland,
I dream about a distant land.

I pull my Aussie hat down low,
Kick back relax before I go.
My eyes are heavy, and life is grand,
I dream about a distant land.

When I awake from silent slumber,
I will leave my home from way down under.
And with a poem and books in hand,
I will fly off to explore, a distant land.

Beyond the Foggy Lens

A desert moon is shining, with a coolness in the air,
Beyond the foggy lens, I gave a Welcomed stare.
Through the haze and blur, a peace within the light,
Gives comfort in the coolness, within the desert night.

No way to clear my vision, here in chilly winds,
No way to make it focus, no way to reach the lens.
In awe I gaze in wonder, what simply can it be?
What lies beyond the blur, what's there I cannot see?

A native voice then tells me, someday you shall return,
Until that time arrives, tell all what you have learned.
The warming light starts fading, it slowly starts to dim,
I know someday I'll see what lies, beyond the foggy lens.

A Haiku for pdenver

The Thrill of The Chase,
Creates memories that last,
Chase your dreams pdenver.

Breathe

With every breath we take, we move closer to our demise,
Live not beyond the shadows, breath through living eyes.
Cease your tears of present eyes, those lost in days gone by,
Reunions do await you, within the midnight sky.

For he who travels a darkened path, filled with lost dismay,
Will drift upon the waters, then quickly float away.
Yesterday is a memory, but tomorrow waits anew,
So, you can breathe the beauty, of life inside of you.

Though our breaths are numbered, breath like there is no end,
Live like yellow leaves, upon an endless wind.
When reunion time arrives and it's time for you to leave,
You'll cherish all the days gone by; proud you chose to breathe.

Camera Shy

Somebody told me, that Fennboree was near,
I'd sure like to make it, out there this year.
But I have a problem, and it is plain to see,
That I do not like the cameras, pointing straight at me.

I'm a little bit shy, in front of a lens,
But it sure would be nice, to meet all my friends.
Desertphile said, he's bringing the wood,
Me I'm debating whether I should.

The campfire will burn, and stories will fly,
With everyone toasting, glasses held high.
There may be a visit, from you know who,
Torn with myself, now what should I do?

I know that the cameras, around there will swarm,
Flashing like lightning, amidst a great storm.
I guess I could go, and stay in my tent,
So, when I get home, I could say that I went.

Decisions, decisions, I one day must make,
For now, I'll just think and take me a break.
I hear Fenboree, is a heck of a blast,
But it's three days for me, just dodging the flash.

A Leprechaun's Ride

High upon the rainbows arc,
Rests a tiny leprechaun.
Gazing up at clouds so dark,
A perfect perch before it's gone.

His climb to get up to its top,
Was slow and tests his will.
Rested up, vowed not stop,
Prepared to slide downhill.

Both hands grab his tall green hat,
He raised his curl toe boots.
He knows below is where it's at,
Then slides down the colored chute.

To ride a magic rainbow,
Is a leprechaun's perfect dream.
To ride upon while colors glow,
To sound, his tiny scream.

When his ride was over,
All the joy his heart could hold,
Landing in a field of clover,
Beside his pot of gold.

Christmas Flames

Sitting by the fireplace, the snow outside it falls,
Christmas is upon us; I've decked my cozy halls.
Soft music in the air, the tune "Oh Holy Night",
My Christmas tree is blinking, with colors bold and bright.

While staring in the fireplace, I hold a glass of wine,
My mind it drifts away, to another place and time.
One cold and starry night, a precious child was born,
They placed him in a manger, a stall out in the barn.

Mary named him Jesus, but little did she know,
How he would change the world, everywhere he'd go.
From feeding many men, on a single tiny fish,
He brought the lame to walk again and given many's wish.

That Christmas gift was special, wrapped up in woven cloth,
Later he would die for us, nailed on a wooden cross.
To give an open doorway, to eternity in peace,
Aloud I thank him for that, I know he hears me speak.

My warming fire just flickers, my glass of wine is low,
Have a Merry, Merry Christmas, I'll say before I go.
Enjoy your time with family, during all your Christmas season,
But don't forget the baby gift, for truly he's the reason.

With my glass held high, I toast to all my friends,
A warm felt Christmas card, to each of you I send.
My fire is burning softly, outside a falling snow,
That's it from me till next time…see ya …I gotta go…

Future Drums

The smoke, the drums, of years ago,
The sounds of a child at play.
A desert life remembered though,
All now, has gone away.

A life enriched by desert lands,
A life so proud to be.
Now lost within the arid sands,
Saved by all who see.

The winds of Time are steady,
Our drum it slowly fades.
A future at the ready,
To seek the life, we've made.

Enjoy it, as you live it,
Your life, that's next to none.
So, futures then can seek it,
Your smoke, your life, your drums.

Grandma

As me and grandma stroll along,
In shortened stride we sing a song.
Hand in hand, my life is good,
Upon a trail, deep in the woods.

The woods are quiet, the wind is still,
We notice something, upon a hill.
While staring through, a gentle fog,
We stop to rest, upon a log.

Grandma turns and says to me,
"You want to go up, there and see?"
And with a nod, I say "I do",
" You lead the way, I'll follow you."

As we climb the foggy rise,
Suspense it quickly, fills our eyes.
Then grandma turns and looks at me,
Amazed at what we both now see.

Ruins from a distant time,
Covered by the green of vines.
Hand in hand we look around,
Through the leaves, upon the ground.

Then I see it, just sitting there,
Me and grandma, stop and stare.
An ancient pot, was made of clay,
Left there from, an ancient day.

Inside the pot, upon the ground,
Amazed what me and grandma found.
A necklace made of turquoise beads,
Just waiting for a boy like me.

Grandma says, "the treasures mine",
" You found it midst these covered vines".
As we leave the foggy hill,
I can't explain, just how I feel.

To find a treasure, that ancients hid,
I sure am one, but lucky kid.
Two treasures I have, the stories I'll tell,
The other is grandma, with me on the trail.

I Stare

I made the flight, from the city lights,
I see it proudly standing there.
The hat of kings, it shines so bright,
With wings tucked in, I stare.

Heavenly Songs

Lia today, may bring you deep sorrow,
But grief it eases, with each passing tomorrow.
I know she walks, with staff in her hand,
Over trails with God, in the promise land.

No pain, no sorrow, no doubt, no fear,
Just joyous times, with him walking near.
My prayers are with you, so Lia be strong,
In silence you will hear, her heavenly songs.

Neighbor Hears the Phantom

Once within a moonless night, I also pondered weak and tired,
With many crinkled maps, spread upon my dusty floor,
I too was plotting on my mapping, then heard the shadow tapping,
Gently in his rapping, tap, tap, tapping, on my neighbor's door.

With my ear pressed to the wall, I too could hear the shadows call,
Oh, but I did hear a tinkling bell, that usually follows up a spell.
Locked my door for my own sake, dim my lights, my measures take.
My ear still pressed against the wall; I hear the bathroom waters fall.

There's a tapping with shadows call, loudest on I've heard of all,
Then silence in the walls so thin, I lost the sound of shadows wind.
Upon my dusty floor once more, pondered on my maps again,
To fill my quest to golden shore, a chest of gold and ancient lore.

The moonless night does slowly pass, no ringing at my neighbors' door,
I chose a path to golden hoard, now peaceful dreams I'm living in
As the morning nears, Bumps on my arms, I feel as if a phantom's near,
Alone I lay and listened well, heard phantom through the windowpane.

Rustling at my neighbors' glass, phantom wails as if to say "now".
Through window crack I did listen, to phantom who explained.
Alone and brave I went by chance, in darkness phantom said,
Worried to be spotted and afraid I ducked my head.

With a swishing of his cape, the winds began to blow,
My neighbors voice was muffled, phantom said "let's go".
Shadow waits at opened door, neighbor slipped into their sneaker,
I feel as if my heart was weaker, no tap, tap tapping on my neighbor's door,

The silence was then broken, the phantom wailed "NO MORE".

Private Treptow 1918

On the 19th day of January, in 1894,
He was born unto this country, a man we all adore.
Way up in Wisconsin, near bloomer I am told,
Is where my hero grew up, and his chilling stories told.

The world was at unrest and times were extremely hard,
In 1917 he joined up with, the Iowa National guards.
World war I was in full swing and now was in his vision,
Once he joined, he became, a soldier in the Rainbow Division.

He served his time as a runner, a carrier of all letters,
Between the Companies, fast he ran, no one could it better.
On the 29th day in the month of July, bullets flew through the skies,
The letter he carried, along the river, could save his brothers lives.

The bullets finally found him, hard he fell to the ground,
Though laying in the battlefield, he could barely hear the sounds.
Then he took his final breath, there on the bank of a river,
The words found written in his diary, when read they'll make you shiver.

A pledge he has written, not wanting no thanks,
Explains why he laid for us, on that riverbank.
Private Treptow he fought for us, until the time he fell,
So, we can live and enjoy the sound, of mighty freedoms bell.

I know that you can see me, I hope this will suffice,
I salute to you brave soldier, for paying the ultimate price.

Newborn Chief

In the year of 1560, in a dry and arid land,
A tiny child was born, in a proud and noble clan.
Navajo by birth and Bidziil he was named,
By elders sitting around, their campfires dancing flames.

Bidziil's cry was loud, within the desert night,
Cradled in her arms, she was fighting for her life.
Upon her face she carried, a newborn painful smile,
She struggled to survive, to hold him for a while.

As the days they passed, she grew stronger by the day,
She knew that she would live, to someday see him play.
Bidziil he was named, "the strong one" on that night,
Proudly for his mother, who did not give up her fight.

As the years they past, Bidziil he grew strong,
Together with his mother, they'd chant their native songs.
Later he became, their strong and noble chief,
Standing for his people, through happiness and grief.

For many, many moons, Bidziil lead with pride,
Many born amongst them, while many elders died.
The campfire it was burning, full moon within the sky,
Then Bidziil heard the sound, of a newborns gentle cry.

He looked up to the heavens, with his hands held high,
Upon his cheek a tear, that's fallen from his eye.
He thanked the mighty spirit, for his years upon this sod,
And for the newborn Chief, just sent to him by God.

One Voice

Two thousand any twenty years ago,
In a dry and arid place.
Mourners let their feelings show,
As blood ran down his face.

Caused by those, an evil choice,
To mute his words of gold.
To stop his true enlightened voice,
And what the future holds.

Though tattered, bruised and weak,
Little air to make a sound.
All mourners heard him speak,
His voice rang all around.

With soldiers' man by man,
And mourners on their knees.
There in those arid sands,
A voice for who believes.

That was many years ago,
His voice still heard today.
Those arid sands, still gently blow,
In that land so far away.

His words will not be muted,
By time, hate or disgrace.
They're firmly heard and rooted,
By the blood upon his face.

Pearly Gates

Wisdom comes in many forms,
Just seek and you will find.
Beyond the walls of daily norms,
Food for your hungered mind.

Use your imagination,
Just travel where it goes.
Enjoy the great sensation,
Of knowledge as it grows.

Your mind it has no limits,
Like trails that slowly fade.
Explore what's deep within it,
You'll love the choice you made.

Take off now my friend,
A brand-new journey waits.
A mind that has no end,
Goes beyond the pearly gates.

Rain

Always when you're feeling down,
Remember what I say.
Without a lonely frown,
The sun would shine all day.

Rain in form of tears,
There on your saddened face.
Would wash away your fears,
Be strong while you embrace.

No matter what you do, remember what I say,
Rainbows need the rain; your tears will go away.

O' Keefe and the Jimson Weed

Look within the sunshine, for I will not be found,
Under rays of moonlight, is where my beauty bounds.
Waiting in the darkness, with blooms as white as snow,
Within the desert night, my evil doesn't show.

You know me as a Jimson Weed, or maybe Devils Snare,
Most of those who know me, really do not care.
Alone here in the darkness, my beauties often missed,
Though I look real tempting, I have an evil kiss.

One night while I was resting, I opened up my blooms,
I see a shadow coming, beneath a full lit moon.
She came and looked upon me, careful not to touch,
Then she started painting, oh she cared so much.

I spread my tiny blooms, as far as they would go,
To help her while she painted, my pedals white as snow.
I knew that she was special, by how she held her brush,
Carefully she painted me, not in a hurried rush.

When she finished painting, I seen her moonlit smile,
Proudly staring at her work, for just a little while.
She gathered up her paints, I see her in the moon,
I hope that she can comet again, sometime very soon.

Even though my poison, scares everyone away,
I'll not forget the night, that painter came my way.
Then she disappears, in the shadows of some trees,
I hope that she has painted, her world known masterpiece.

Penning machine

I walk into my workshop, I then turn on the lights,
Sitting right before me, you won't believe your eyes.
This machine is incredibly special, I purchased from a lad,
To me it's so unique, so many lights it has.

I walk across my workshop, turn on its power switch,
It begins to rumble, shake and wildly twitch.
Then it settles down, now purring like a kitten,
I open up its ink well, blue ink is what it's getting.

Then I walk around the front, to its panel switches,
Pushed the big green button, I almost crapped my britches.
Papers started flying, shooting from the top,
I quickly hit the red button, hoping it would stop.

The papers kept on flying, they lay across the floor,
High up in the air, they're continuing to soar.
Then I reached and picked up, a paper at my feet,
The words on it were blue and were addressed to me.

As I carefully read the words, this is what it said,
"Come out west for healing dirt", then I scratched my head.
It was signed jdiggins, no other words at all,
I'll clean this mess up later, adventure awaits us all.

I leave my shop and close the door, the stories I will share.
And I'll grab an extra shovel, so I can have a spare.

My Warm Necklace

The sky is partly cloudy, white clouds just hanging there,
Slowly drifting to the east, as if to get somewhere.
Me I sit upon a log, I've been hiking all day long,
Listening to the symphony, of nature's lovely song.

I'm looking at a mighty Cliff, the rocks rise in the sky,
The water is free falling, as if it tried to fly.
Splashing at the bottom, the mist filled natures air,
In awe I sit and stared at it, so thankful I was there.

I had to get a closer look, I raised up to my feet,
Walked over to the waterfall, the mist it fell on me.
That is when it happened, the mist began to part,
Me I felt a warmness, deep feelings in my heart.

Then an ancient Indian girl, showed her face to me,
She was smiling in her spirit, happy as can be.
She told me that they lived, right there along the creek,
In the sounds of a rushing waterfall, I clearly heard her speak.

She tells me of a winter, so awfully long ago,
And how a blizzard trapped them, within the blinding snow.
For weeks, the snow fell on them, no one could see the sun,
Her tribe began just dying off, one by precious one.

She tells me of a necklace, in which she proudly wore,
She placed it in a crevice, along this rocky shore.
Then her spirit drifted, slowly down the bank,
Then pointed at a crevice and said I owe no thanks.

I peeked into the crevice, I seen it laying there,
Just like she had placed it, in her winter of despair.
Then her spirit disappeared, just faded in the mist,
I held her stunning necklace, gently in my fist.

I look up to the heavens, I thanked her for her gift,
Thanked her for her time, there at that mighty Cliff.
The warmness in my heart, it never went away,
Since I touched the necklace, in the rocks that sunny day.

I know my ancient friend, will forever be with me,
When I close my eyes, her face I clearly see.
White clouds above are drifting and I start heading back,
With a warmness in my heart, and her necklace around my neck.

Past Rivers

The search is ever endless,
Past rivers deep and wide.
Is long ago within us,
Alive down deep inside?

Take a day and set aside,
Time to go explore.
To find what out there surly lies,
Look and look some more.

And tune your ears into the wind,
Listen for their whispered word.
For if you do this, trust me friend,
It is amazing what is heard.

Small Town County Fair

In calm of summers evening air,
Many come to see.
Lights strung at the county fair,
Within the mighty trees.

The Ferris wheel is shining,
Lit spokes within its wheel.
Its riders are admiring,
This fair upon the hill.

A scream it fills the air,
From the nearby Crazy Spin.
A huge brown teddy bear,
Hangs for you to win.

Hot dogs for a dollar,
Cotton candy on a stick.
Kids they run and holler,
Deciding which to pick.

BB guns are firing,
By boys and dads alike.
The fishing pond's inspiring,
Poles held by little tykes.

It's a grand ole summer night,
With a moon high in the air.
Oh, the memories, sounds and sights,
Of our small-town County Fair.

Cowboys Home

Been riding on a dusty trail, my horse and me alone,
Looking for a special town, that I can call my home.
Many years I've traveled, I've entered many towns,
Just to ride on through them, always feeling down.

The sun is hot, my hat is wet, my saddle dry and squeaks,
Up ahead I see a town, first one I've seen in weeks.
Maybe I can get a bath and start my life anew,
My horse could use a blacksmith, he's missing one back shoe.

The town is getting closer, with every step we take,
There's something written up ahead, upon a wooden stake.
I sit up in the saddle, to read what it might say,
Upon the stake is written, the town name Santa Fe.

As I ride into this town, the folks just stare at me,
With my pistol on my side, I was dusty as can be.
I rode up to a hitching post, then swung down off my horse,
Suddenly a stranger spoke, his voice was rough and coarse.

"Welcome stranger to our town", "we call this Santa Fe".
" Are you just passing through", "or do you plan to stay"?
Then he offered me a drink, on him in their saloon,
And told me where to grab a bite, over at the greasy spoon.

The people there were genuinely nice, everywhere I stopped,
The hotel where I stayed the night and even the blacksmith shop.
My dusty trail has ended, I think I've found my home,
I think I'll stay in Santa Fe and rest my aching bones.

A week has passed since I arrived, at this special place,
But I have yet to feel a smile, upon my wrinkled face.
I dream of all the sunsets, that I've seen along the trail,
Just My horse and me alone, no words can even tell.

I'm packing up my saddlebags, I'm leaving at first light,
This cowboy got to leave this town, to me it doesn't feel right.
I've got to have my open space, no walls to close me in,
With Santa Fe behind me, my trail to home begins.

My saddle it's still squeaking, the sun is getting hot,
This cowboy sure is thankful, for everything I've got.
While riding along the Rio Grande, I look up to the sky,
Thank you, God, this trails my home, I'll ride it till I die.

December 20th, 1968

Time slows, a mind in wander,
A vision, life over yonder.
Streaks beneath the thunders boom,
Like lightning fills this lonesome room.

In thought the visions are still so real,
The lack of sleep, a hurried meal.
To hear the sounds, of way back then,
As lead impacts into the tin.

Yellow flashing with blinks of red,
The canopy cracks just overhead.
Levers pulled a force of wind,
Up and out was this the end.

A fire upon the mountainside,
On wind to drift alone to glide.
To step upon Gods precious ground,
Surrounded by the jungles sound.

Awake so long through worried night,
Waiting for the morning light.
Calls were made, wave of the hands,
Smiles upon the Candy Ann.

A cable ride in treetops brash,
Up and away the chopper flashed.
Two days later to leave that place,
At Temples door, smiles on their face.

Bubba's Porch

In the Chase I feel I'm Focused; I live it deep within,
And I just had to take a trip, to see where it began.
As I arrived in Temple, passed the city limits sign,
The sky above was clear, the sun it brightly shined.

Construction it was hectic, But I did not fall in defeat,
Determined I continued, right on down Main Street.
As I drove the final block, the lot was just ahead,
Quotes of Forrest entered, and bounced within my head.

Then on my right I seen it, proudly standing tall,
The old front porch of Forrest Fenn, I listened as it called.
I parked along the roadside, not caring who was near,
I followed the sounds now calling, that whispered in my ear.

Then I sat upon the porch, and gently closed my eyes,
Who knew when it was poured, it would touch so many lives?
Finally, I was sitting, at the place it all began,
The childhood home of one great man, we know as Forrest Fenn.

Then all at once it happened, I could not believe my eyes,
When I slowly opened them, a vision to my surprise.
The year was 1935, the house it stood alone,
An old black car in the drive, I knew someone was home.

Then the screen door opened, and Bubba he walked out,
A toy in each hand, with a sour little pout.
He sat upon the top step, just looking right at me,
His vision was so real, I felt as if he sees.

Bubba he just sat there, I could see it in his eyes,
He would do great things, to change some people's lives.
After just a little bit, his mama she spoke out,
"Bubba come and eat", I heard her softly shout.

Then bubba he got up and headed for the door,
Then he turned and paused and looked at me once more.
The screen door slammed behind him; his vision just fades away.
I'm thankful to have seen, Bubba come outside to play.

I raised up to my feet, with one final look around,
Got into my car and left his old hometown.
If you go to see the place, where the chase for sure began,
And sit upon the porch, of childhood Forrest Fenn.

I hope you too have visions; I wish you all the best,
Maybe our trails will cross, while seeking Bubba's chest.
If that never happens, I just want to say,
I will never forget my time with Bubba, sitting on his porch to play.

Do It Again

Halts,
Faults,
Down,
Brown.
Keep a smile and never frown.

Meek,
Seek,
Nigh,
Sly.
Forrest Fenn's one good ole guy.

Creek,
Speak,
Loads,
Toads.
We all have traveled many roads.

Maze,
Blaze,
Wise,
Prize.
The look of adventure within our eyes.

Gaze,
Phase,
Spin,
Win.
when the Chase is over, let's do it again.

Halt and Listen

In season chilled, rich snowflakes glisten,
Search thee soul, through moon lit night.
Tune ye ears, just halt and listen,
Hear the North Star, shining bright.

Though turned away, from warmth of inn,
Straw and hay, a baby's manger,
Crisp cold of night, one life begins,
Three traveled far, in midst of danger.

Followed bright, a northern star,
Gifts for a newborn, mighty King.
Tired of travel, they came afar,
Knelt in his stable, the angels sing.

Life of a King, moved quickly by,
Spreading good, across the lands.
Sentenced while, the faithful cry,
Rusty nails, through savior's hands.

Thorns that pierce, his mighty head,
Blood that fell, upon the ground.
Silence covers, his face of red,
Upon a hill, of a nearby town.

To rise again, with heavens power,
Open door, for you and me.
If in our hearts, our finest hour,
With him we'll, forever be.

In season chilled, rich snowflakes glisten,
Search thee soul, just halt and listen.

If I Could Only Back Up Time

You said you'd love me, till you died,
Oh, how I wish, you meant it all.
But I know now, to me you lied,
As your leaving, down the hall.

You didn't shed, a single tear,
Though they swelled, within my eyes.
Where did it go, so many years?
Just to end up, with goodbye.

If I could only, back up time,
Oh, the things I would have done.
I'd give this broke olé, heart of mine,
All to you, my only one.

As I sit here, on the bed,
I hear the slamming, of the door.
Echo sounds, of things you said,
Your never coming, back no more.

I hear the silence, all alone,
In this lonely, house of mine.
I know now, your surely gone,
If I could only, back up time.

If I could only, back up time,
Oh, the things I would have done.
I'd give this ole' heart of mine,
All to you, my only one.

If I could only, back up time,
Oh, the things I would have done.

Old Top Hat

On a sheet of paper, written down, the poem of Forrest Fenn,
Line by line, I cut it up, in strips and threw it in.
An old top hat, that I had found, many years ago,
Added in some potion and stirred it awfully slow.

Soon bubbles started rising, slowly to the top,
The magic book I'm reading from, say's stir and do not stop.
Just a little longer, the smoke began to rise,
From the old top hat, that holds the clues, burnt my watering eyes.

The magic book now tells me, too slowly let it cool.
I hope this really works for me, if not I look a fool.
Fingers crossed, hopes are high, no telling what I'd see,
An hour later, which seemed to me, like eternity.

The time has come to strain my mix, and let magic do the trick,
I stirred it one last final time, with my wooden stick.
I strained it off, to my surprise, the strips, what the heck?
I felt my hair begin to rise, at the bottom of my neck.

All the strips joined as one, in the bottom of the hat,
Folded up, unharmed at all, if you can believe in that.
I reached inside the old top hat, grabbed the folded sheet,
Wondered what I'd see inside, victory or defeat?

Unfolded that piece of paper, that once held the clues of Fenn,
Dropped my head and closed my eyes, it read,
" Warm Water Halts is where you begin".

The Reason

Sitting by the fireplace, the snow outside it falls,
Christmas is upon us; I've decked my cozy halls.
Soft music in the air, the tune Oh Holy Night,
My Christmas tree is blinking, multiple colors bright.

While staring in the fireplace, with my glass of wine,
My mind it drifts away, to another place and time.
One cold and starry night, a precious child was born,
They placed him in a manger, a stall out in the barn.

Mary named him Jesus, but little did she know,
How he would change the world, everywhere he'd go.
From feeding a thousand men, on a single tiny fish,
Brought the lame to walk and given many's wish.

That Christmas day was special, Jesus wrapped in cloth,
Later he would die for us, nailed upon a cross.
To give an open doorway, to eternity in peace,
Aloud I thank him for that, I know he hears me speak.

My warming fire just flickers, my glass of wine is low,
Have a Merry, Merry Christmas, I'll say before I go.
Enjoy your time with family, during your Christmas season,
But don't forget the baby because Jesus he's the reason.

With my glass held high, a toast to all my friends,
A warm felt Christmas card, to each of you I send.
My fire is burning softly, outside a heavy snow,
That's it from me till next time, see ya I gotta go.

Within the Trees

The autumn leaves, so yellow bright,
Upon the wind, they take to flight.
To ride upon, the chilly breeze,
In mountains deep, no eyes to see.

A flight so short, they tumble down,
To rest upon, a covered ground.
Silent and still, on bed of gold,
Waiting for what, the winter holds.

Then trees so bare, white aspens bark,
Reflect the moon, within the dark.
Awaiting in, the winter snows,
For warmth of spring when aspens grow.

Please take the time, enjoy the cold,
Admire what nature, has to hold.
Go rest within, the Golden leaves,
And find your peace, within the trees.

World of Unknown

Fear not what lies, in a world of unknown,
For with each step, you boldly take.
You'll discover the seeds, you've already sown,
A decision that's yours and fearless you make.

The dark will then lighten, your path up ahead,
Your fear will subside, and courage will grow.
Then knowing unknowns, won't seem quite as bad,
Enjoying your journey, as onward you go.

Just hear me as, one friend to another,
Brave is within you, the decisions your own.
A bright world awaits now, for you to discover,
Enjoy your journey, to your world of unknown.

Rewards

The time we spend, upon this earth,
Reward us every day.
Is there more than daily worth,
Not nurtured on our way.

In your very family tree,
The branches tend to grow.
Fruit I know you surely see,
You cherish them as you go.

Reap the fruit of children,
It's in your very reach.
In your harvest let them shine,
The children have a speech.

Seeds will keep on dropping,
You'll become an older branch,
Sow your seeds while stopping,
Our children deserve a chance.

Holy Child

The day was kind of gloomy, the sky was overcast,
I was walking through a pueblo, of the distant past.
At the ground I looked, as I slowly strolled alone,
Looking for some arrowheads, that I can call my own.

I went into the kiva, the walls were perfectly round,
That is where I found it, just lying on the ground.
A perfect little cross, it was so slightly stained,
As I gently rubbed it, engraved I seen a name.

Ashkii Dighin was the name, upon the tiny cross,
It once belonged to him, for centuries it's been lost.
I reached into my pocket, pulled out my new cell phone,
To find out what the name meant before I headed home.

All at once the clouds, they parted in the sky,
The sun rays shined upon me, glaring in my eyes.
Then I heard his voice, speaking from the glare,
Ashkii Dighin spoke to me, all I could do was stare.

He said his name meant holy child and he was Navajo,
This place was once his home, many, many years ago.
He said the cross was blessed, by elders in the past,
Smudged by smoke and holy dirt, forever it would last.

He said to take it home with me, and keep it close at heart,
Believe in what your holding, it'll take you mighty far.
Then the clouds rejoined, the sky again was Grey,
I felt that I found solitude, on the ground that day.

Forever I will cherish, I'll share my cross with smiles,
Stained from years ago, by a gracious holy child.
Before I left the kiva, I knelt upon my knees,
I thanked Ashkii Dighin, for, the cross he's given me.

As I walked back to my truck, the sky still overcast,
The cross clamped tightly in my fist, my gift from ancient past.
I could barely wait, to drive back into town,
So, I could share with all, the precious cross That I have found.

Farewell

I once was here but now I'm gone,
In search of trails to walk upon.
To share the peace within myself,
So, others can reap my inner wealth.

My Memories made in days gone past,
A thousand dreams will forever last.
Until the day my soul does fly,
I'll ask the solemn question why?

Those answers I may never know,
But peace on earth's the seeds I'll sow.
To friends I've made upon my trail,
Deep in my heart I bid farewell.

Crystal Bridges

Over crystal bridges, my journey to unknown,
I walk upon the air, where many others flown.
High above the clouds, I see them far below,
Just like a bunch cotton, gleaming white as snow.

The light that shines upon me, more soothing than the sun,
Memories I reflect on, recounting one by one.
Then high above the mountains, with White upon their top,
Slowly I walk to them, I take some time to stop.

I gaze down on the mountains, their solitude and peace,
A warmness then embraced me, like wrapped in woven fleece.
As I stroll along, my heart it speaks to me,
Walking over vastness, of a deep blue shining sea.

Then the light in dims, just like the setting of the sun,
On air I keep on walking, to where it all begun.
My journey over clouds and many distant ridges,
In awe I slowly walk, back over crystal bridges.

A Single Seed

Life is like a planted seed, when nourished it will grow,
Is a seed less pampered, still apt to live and glow?
A single seed's important, each and every one,
Game of life depends on, them growing in the sun.

Of course, all seeds are needed, in this game of life we play,
Poker or a game of chess, one seed could save the day.
Happiness is our final goal, as our seed begins to grow,
Are the seeds around us, also ready to make their show?

The seed begins to slowly rise, making its first debut,
Pot of clay enhances its overall lovely view.
Fate it plays a special part, while the small seed starts to rise,
Deals to it the sun and rain, from up within the skies.

You watch the plant grow larger, proud and standing tall,
Four seasons later fully grown, admired by each and all.
Cards to place within the pot, so others will know its name,
And let it have its glory, and proudly show its fame.

A seed it has a special roll, like cards within a deck,
Joker may hold the highest rank, but to all it is just a speck.
You may think at different times, your seeds not going to grow,
Play your part and nourish it, I promise you it will glow.

Whether your seed is young, or your seed has fully grown,
You have the means within you, your heart has always known.
Like the world around you, your happiness will shine through,
It all begins with a tiny seed, that lives deep inside of you.

Or is it all the other seeds, that you should nourish too?
Not to focus on just your seed, beautiful gardens begin with two.

Clean Slate

I came into this world so frail, blank slate in which to write,
Loved ones wrote the first few words, with caring chalk of white.
Words were small and simple, my mind was very young,
From that moment forward, my eager mind begun.

Beside my growing mind of slate, an eraser you would find,
To remove unwanted words of Grey, not needed in my mind.
Decade past, my slate has grown, my mind is taking shape,
Nourished by the ones who care, still writing on my slate.

Word by word, my list grew long, with each passing year,
Speaking words of wisdom, to those who want to hear.
Many, many years have passed, my hair is turning Grey,
On my slate, a million words since that fragile day.

Now sitting in a waiting room, for my grandchild, I do wait,
To come into this world so frail, and with an empty slate.
Simple words I've chosen, and with my chalk in hand,
To write upon an empty slate, that's tender and so grand.

Time has come, to write my words, first words to start anew,
Gently with my chalk of white, I write" I Love You ".
Beside my growing grandchild, I'll walk throughout the years,
Oh, the stories I will tell, to fill those tender ears.

We all have words of wisdom, written on our slate of time,
Take a moment, choose some words, and pass them down the line.
Help a growing, slate of words, begin a brand-new start,
If you do this, Trust in me, you'll feel it in your heart.

Family Treasures

Mist in a meadow of green, dew upon my boots,
Searching for my past, home of ancestor roots.
Alone I tramp in memory, old letters in my hand,
She talks about the creek and the rolling of the land.

In words she spills her memories, neath a huge oak tree,
On a handmade blanket, she was happy as can be.
Up ahead I see the tree, it's very large in size,
Then I finally seen it, I can't believe my eyes.

The rocks looked like a monument, where the house had stood,
So happy that I found it, I wondered if I could.
I sat upon a flat rock, that use to be her steps,
Staring at the chimney, the inside was jet black.

I reached into my pocket, one final note from her,
She talks about her family, and the fighting that occurred.
And how they fought them off, with every ounce they tried,
One by one her family fell, to the floor and died.

She gathered up their valuables, placed in an old tin box,
And hid them in the fireplace, beneath the blackened rocks.
I looked up to the fireplace, I felt her presence there,
Afraid to go and look, all I could do was stare.

Now the sun is high, and the mist has gone away,
I found the courage to look, I bowed my head and prayed.
The picture in the letter, shows each and every stone,
Two rocks from the front, is where her box is shown.

Standing by the fireplace, I see the rock she tells,
Gently I removed it, then to my knees I fell.
An old tin box before me, from years and years ago,
I feel my ancestors near me, I feel as if they know.

I opened up the box, wonder filled my eyes,
I felt just like a two-year-old, with their Cracker Jack surprise.
The box was filled with coins, a pocket watch lay on the top,
Right beside a locket, I knelt there at that spot.

I open the old locket, two pictures I see inside,
my great, great grandmother Elsie, the other her husband Clyde.
Grandpa Clyde was holding, the watch from way back then,
Grandma Elsie was wearing, her locket with a grin.

I do believe they know that family found their box,
Hidden for years and years, inside these family rocks.
I say my words of thanks, to my ancestors of long ago,
I pause beside the oak tree, last look before I go.

You have family too, their way back in your roots,
Maybe you should visit them, get mist upon your boots.
An old home place awaits you; it needs you standing there,
Please take the time to show, your ancestors that you care.

The sun has disappeared, I have no time to stall,
While leaving I hear the sound, of a hoot owl's lonely call.

Game of Life

Fear not the shadows, embrace the dark,
At Dawns first light, the twilight looms.
For voices in your soul does hark,
Speaking like a thunders boom.

He who listens, from deep within,
Can shed some light and see afar.
In midst of darkness, where tales are grim,
Rays do twinkle, like distant stars.

In silence midst your inner thinking,
In conversation with yourself.
Fear not the darkness, stars are blinking,
Find some courage on your inner shelf.

Alone within you changes made,
Rejoicing while your voices hark,
Fearing not what lies within the shade,
Brave you'll be, within the dark.

Live a life, where deeds are good,
Embrace it with a grin,
Treat all others like you should,
In your game of life, you'll win.

First Aid Kit

Walking through the desert, sand beneath my feet,
My steps are getting slower, dragging from the heat.
The sun is high above me, there is no wind at all,
In my ears I hear, the vultures as they call.

Lost out in this desert, I need to find some shade,
I mumble to myself, about choices I have made.
Up ahead I see a rock, where I can rest my legs,
This heat is going to kill me, help me God I beg.

I know that I am in this mess, all because of me,
I walked into this desert, not prepared as I should be.
I know that I may surely die, here in this desert sand,
Reach out God and help me, I need your guiding hand.

I continued walking, then to my knees I fell,
Slumped and looking down, I do not want to fail.
Then suddenly I feel a breeze, brush across my cheek,
Alone here in the desert, a voice begins to speak.

" Raise up to your feet child and take my helping hand".
"Close your eyes and follow me, I'll lead you from this sand".
I raised up to my feet, the cool wind starts to blow,
With all my faith in God I walked, where his voice told me to go.

I stumbled through the desert sand, with his guiding touch,
"Why me lord?" I asked, "why would you care so much?"
Then I topped a gentle rise, and I was looking down,
Staring at the cars go by, within a busy town.

The tears fill up my eyes, they're running down my cheek,
I survived the desert because I listened to God speak.
Even though I felt alone, there was always two,
If you're in your desert, he's also there with you.

If you're going hiking, please always go prepared,
It will surely help you, when your alone and scared.
Take some time to ponder, right there where you sit,
God's the most important thing, in your first aid kit.

Gone Fishing

My pole is all ready, new line on the spool,
My fly box is loaded, so ready to fool.
My waders they hang, with feet in the air,
My net hangs beside them, so ready to snare.

My hat on a hook, my vest hanging near,
In silence the water, it's ripples I hear.
An image I see, it's been burned in my brain,
A great peaceful morning, no forecast of rain.

A stroke of my rod, my line softly lay,
Atop of the current and moving away.
A twitch of my rod, my tongue in my cheek,
A quick sudden jerk, the one that I seek.

My heart is all in it, my visions are true,
I dream of the water and a sky that is blue.
It warms me to feel, the chase and the bite,
While outside the grounds, all covered in white.

The Pawn

The game of life is set, all players in a row,
One but tiny pawn, the very first to go.
Reluctant pawns they move, one space at a time,
The eager pawns move twice, advance their battle line.

A bishop slides across, to take a troubled horse,
Life's battle it has started, all players stay on course.
Think of what you're doing, the consequence is huge,
One false move and then, from this game you are removed.

The rook shows little mercy, just sweeping to and from,
Attacking one by one and smiling as he goes.
I am a tiny pawn, all alone it seems,
One by one they fall, to protect our mighty king.

The horses take the pawns, their queen falls to our rook,
We lost our last brave bishop; too bad he didn't look.
The game is nearly over, two kings and tiny me,
Space by space he moves, not watching as he flees.

My king he sits back smiling, I have him on the run,
Right into the corner, of where my game begun.
I'm just a tiny pawn, but I make my final move,
Their king just stands there gazing, with nothing left to prove.

He lays his crown upon the board and takes his final space.
Captured by me a pawn, a smile upon my face.
If you feel belittled, or your life's not worth a thing,
Please think about the pawn, who took the mighty king.

Stallion Heart

While riding through the desert, I seen him standing there,
Head up high and staring, beside him stood his mare.
This stallion was a beauty, he was strawberry roan,
If I could ever rope him, I'd try to take him home.

Then one day while riding, I was resting by a rock,
I see the stallion coming, with his lovely stock.
I dallied up my rope, three wraps around the horn,
Loop in hand I waited, he's going to be a storm.

I knew my throw was crucial, I only had one shot,
Around my head one time, then I gave it all I've got.
I looped the mighty stallion and yes, he was a storm,
With my horse he drug me, through the cactus's and thorns.

When we finished spinning, he stood and looked at me,
As we rode back to the house, he was skittish as can be.
Day by day I worked with him, I slowly gained his trust,
With a saddle on his back, it's time to break or bust.

I led him from the round pen, into the desert red,
The room I knew I needed; his ears laid on his head.
My left foot in the stirrup, left hand upon the horn,
I swing my right foot over, it's time to ride the storm.

He didn't disappoint me, he blew up like a bomb,
With one hand I had the reins, gripped tightly in my palm.
We bucked around the desert, me and that strawberry roan,
Then he finally gave in, we ran back to my home.

That's been twenty years ago, I've rode him every day,
Oh, the miles we've covered, in work and also play.
No money could ever buy him, he has no price at all,
This stallion is my best friend, he's at my beckon call.

I know our days are numbered, and someday we must part,
Until then I know I'll never replace, this stallion in my heart.

The Surprise Catch

In the year of 1826, I lived upon this land,
A hunter for my people, a proud and noble clan.
Alone I spent my days, in search of daily food,
Others they would gather, many piles of wood.

One day while I was hunting, and grasping to my spear,
I heard some distant thunder; I knew the rain was near.
The sky was getting darker, the woods they did the same,
I heard the mighty spirit, just calling out my name.

I walked into a clearing, beside a waterfall,
While looking to the heavens, again I hear his call.
The mighty spirit tells me, to look within the pool,
It was then I noticed, how the fish was plentiful.

I gently raised my spear, and focused on a fish,
Quickly I released it, oh how the water splashed.
One by one I speared the fish, until my bag was full,
Leaving some for next time, here in this tiny pool.

I look up to the heavens, I thank the mighty spirit,
Again, the thunder rumbles, telling me he hears it.
I leave the tiny creek and head back to my clan,
To share my daily catch, with all my fellow man.

Some days when the animals, dodge my sharpened eyes,
A hunter must adapt and return with a surprise.
Today I paused and listened, to a spirit so much higher,
Tonight, we all can eat some fish, while sitting around our fires.

Tomorrow when I rise, I'll go and hunt again,
Today I'll say goodbye, to you my fellow friends.

Winter Home

In trance a lonely chipmunk stares, with ears trained up a ahead,
Pausing from his chores of fall, preparing his winter bed.
A noise within the forest, has broken the silent sound,
His jaws clamped rather tightly, on a twig that he has found.

In suspense he waits and listens, leaves fall from nearby trees,
Until the danger passes, or until the noise he sees.
Time it slowly passes, with no danger seen at all,
He scurries to a rockslide, in the brisk winds of the fall.

Time and time again, he goes down in the hole,
A home it soon will be when winter winds are cold.
His chipmunk days are busy, his awareness stands alert,
A few more trips with pine nuts, he knows it wouldn't hurt.

Winter in the mountains, then comes with no surprise,
North winds start to blow, and snowflakes fill the sky.
But one tiny little chipmunk, cares not the wind that blows,
He's nestled in the rockslide, all cozy in his hole.

The Package

I was an inner-city kid, just past the age of ten,
A package I was given, to deliver just for them.
Not knowing what it was, I took it anyway,
To the place they wanted, to a man called Crazy 8.

As I walked up to him, my fear I couldn't erase,
Below his eye a teardrop, tattooed upon his face.
Crazy 8 just stared at me, his hand beneath his shirt,
I laid the package on the ground, I thought it wouldn't hurt.

Then I turned to walk away, not a word was said,
Then all at once the bullets, whistled above my head.
In fear I took off running, not caring where I went,
I knew then I was used, for a deadly errand sent.

Then all at once I felt it, a burning in my side,
A bullet chased and found me, there in that street I died.
You ask me why I'm telling this, I'll tell the reason why,
Because many kids are living, their inner city lives.

To them I want to say, the choice belongs to you,
You have your life before you and know what you should do.
The package it's not cool, they really do not care,
Please don't be the next one, to stop bullets through the air.

Someday when your old and living far away,
Your thoughts of me will visit, you'll thank me on that day.
And take your faith along, it'll help you on your path,
Don't give in and fall, to drugs all bloody wrath.

I have a package for you, please hold it close and tight,
Then proudly make a drop for me, spread Gods love tonight.
You'll feel it in your heart, just knowing that you could,
Your life will be a long one, while in your faith you stood.

Tribute to Glen Campbell

"By The time I Get to Phoenix", the sun it will be down,
Glen's songs the keep me going, with my hammer down.
Through open lands of Kansas, the traffic starts to slow,
A "Wichita Lineman" is working, high upon the pole.

I'm headed for "A Better Place", tomorrow I should find,
A place that I'll call home, is "Gentle on My Mind".
"I Guess I'm Dumb" for leaving, others say so too,
I roam around this country, in search of someplace new.

I started down in "Galveston", south Texas was my home,
I was a "Rhinestone Cowboy", who needed time to roam.
"These Days" behind the wheel, tomorrow will done,
Once I reach ole Phoenix, I'll live in desert sun.

The sun has finally set, these "Southern Nights" are warm,
Window down and blowing, across my naked arm.
Phoenix now before me, it's signs upon a post,
Home at last, grin on my face, see you "Adios".

Widow of A Hero

Please let me have my time, I'll do it all alone,
Take a wreath of memory, to my soldier who is gone.
A hero fell for all, my hero to be exact,
Moment lost in time, never to come back.

In a giant cemetery, with thousands of white stones,
Silence in my ears, as I walk alone.
To the row of 36, the plot of 104,
Honor in my heart, I miss you even more.

Our lives continue on, without you standing here,
Fallen you may be, your voice I often here.
Soldiers of a country, because of you I'm free,
Thanks, my special hero, for your life you've given me.

The Journey

If a rainbow ends with a pot of gold,
You would chase it till; you are old.
Should you ever, find the pot,
Ever no more, your journey forgot.

Think of others, while riches you found,
Of those less fortunate, scattered abound.
Me I would help, some people in need,
A family who struggles, just needing a seed.

Thousands of wishes, I'd try to fulfill,
Years of struggle, climbing uphill.
From me I would help them, that is my choice,
Now when I speak, they will hear my voice.

Ring out louder than ever before,
My voice will echo from shore to shore.
Bell it sits up high in a steeple,
So loudly it rings, while I help out some people.

I know the rainbow, for its colors so bold,
Will benefit many, with its pot of gold.
To know that the treasure lies within,
At the end of the rainbow, my journey begins.

Wings

Jdiggins there's a story, I think you'd like to hear.
About a certain angel, that evil truly feared.
He was a one-winged angel, one wing upon his back.
Even though he's different, he truly had the knack.

He'd fly around in circles, beautiful artwork in his trust.
Spiraling up into the clouds, trailing angel dust.
All the angels loved him, though he only had one wing.
They'd stop to Hoover in one place, while watching they would sing.

Cheering on that one wing angel, graceful in his art.
You can hear them singing Jdiggins if you listen from your heart.
When my day does come, and I meet the mighty King.
You bet I'm going to tell him that, this angel wants one wing.

The White Buffalo

She came to give her guidance,
To peace and harmony,
Her spirit breaks the silence,
And speaks so soft to me.

She says she's brought a gift,
Of music for all man.
A flute she gently lifts,
Held soft between her hands.

High upon a gentle rise,
The music from her hands.
Rode the wind in prairie skies,
Across the open land.

She said she had one final gift,
To leave here with all man.
And with her pointed finger lifts,
And points across the land.

A herd of bison grazing,
It soothed my aching soul,
To see that was amazing,
One pure and white as snow.

My spirit friend then left me,
In music on the knoll.
In the peace, love and harmony,
Of a lone white Buffalo.

Whispered There

Secrets, secrets, alone in there,
Locked away, in midnights air.
Silent, silent, a voice unheard,
No whispers speak, a sacred word.

Ticks, ticks, the time so fast,
It's chimes ring loud, like distant past.
Live, live, Today so grand,
Enjoy the fellowship of man.

Dream, dream, of future shores,
No ticks to hear, forevermore.
Fly, fly, through midnight air,
To hear the secrets, that's whispered there.

The Best of The Best

Our own world, fun and shining bright,
Energetic, full of colored dreams.
Dimmed by chaos, darkened by fright,
What once was, so distant it seems.

Together is no more, apart we fight chaos,
Unseen, but knowingly there.
Mourning, desperate, so many lost,
Grief upon our sleeves we wear.

But yet we fight, strive and carry on,
Knowing not, living, with utmost care.
Dreams change, adjust, we act upon,
Instinct, survival with no time to spare.

Together as one, we stand, grieve, rejoice,
We'll defeat chaos, regain, dreams of our past.
Flush away the dim, be heard, one united voice,
We'll echo round, a world so large and vast.

Our own world, fun and shining bright,
Family, friends, as once we knew.
Will resume, flourish, within the light,
Hopes, our colored dreams renewed.

Be strong, determined, to fight the fight,
Call on friends, share your will.
Encourage, embrace, share your might,
Upon them, let your courage spill.

Hugs, kisses, freedom to love,
High fives, low fives, all around.
Prayers, sent to the man above,
Handshakes, without gloves abound.

The future will be bright, fun, and caring,
When chaos, in distant past, rests.
From me, Focused, prayers I'm sharing,
I wish for you, my friends, the best of the best.

Grey

Life may not be pleasant, all 24 hours a day,
Can't we just keep the good, and throw the bad away?
It is the diversity around us, with our wounds and battle scars,
That defines us as a person and shows others who we are.

Our lives are not as simple, like the colors black and white,
There is evil living among us, trying to wrong the right.
Pdenver your words ring true, yes, everything you say,
But you would not be you, without your memories of Grey.

Moonlit Answers

Through chill of a moonlit winter night,
I traipse these lonely woods.
While snow does softly end its flight,
Upon my winter hood.

Not knowing what I search for,
I feel it deep within.
The questions in my soul,
Are somewhere deep within.

I stop and gaze behind me,
My tracks are in the snow.
White rests on the naked trees,
Now onward I must go.

Before me snow just glistens,
Moonlight shines the way.
Deep in my soul I listen,
And continue on my way.

I see a bluff before me,
Just feeling I was right.
Climb up to look and see,
What's calling me tonight.

A cavern is before me,
The moon shines slightly in.
An ancient home of Cherokee,
They used it way back when.

A fire ring is before me,
With drawings on the walls,
I feel as if they're with me,
I hear their native calls.

Then to my knees I fall,
Alone but with my friends,
The Cherokee they would tell,
How life it was back then.

When they finished talking,
It was time for me to go,
So onward I start walking,
Back in the mountain snow.

I feel I found the answers,
From My friends of long ago,
Answers I was needing,
To the questions in my soul.

Hearts Eyes

To many times, visions pass,
See it, then it's gone.
Life's within a looking glass,
Treasures sought are none.

You look across the distance,
Must feel there is a prize.
First use your self-persistence,
Look with not your eyes.

Through your heart believing,
Your visions will be best.
Hearts are made for seeing,
Eyes within your chest.

Life Is So Much Better

It's the little things that matter most,
Enjoy them day to day.
A bluebird perched upon a post,
Before it flies away.

Dewdrops on the flowers,
The sunshine on your face.
The evenings golden hour,
As nighttime takes its place.

Like children in a playground,
Carefree running wild.
A gentle breeze that blows around,
And the comfort in a smile.

The little things surround us,
Just look and you will find.
Please pause and take the moment,
And notice time to time.

The sounds of nearby whippoorwills,
And fireflies in the night.
The frost upon your windowsill,
And stars up in the sky.

Fresh bread in the oven,
The smell of summer rain.
Young ones and their shoving,
In their weekly soccer game.

The list goes on and on, my friend,
They're waiting to be seen.
Life is so much better when,
You notice the little things.

Short and Sweet

Take life slow,
Live not fast.
Feel your soul,
Explore your past.

Dig down deep,
Within yourself.
Take a peek,
Your inner self.

Share your heart,
Live not fast.
Some will dart,
Some will bask.

Enjoy all things,
within your reach.
Let it ring,
Do not preach.

Heart will feel,
Shiny brand new.
Let love spill,
Inside of you.

Enjoy your time,
Each passing minute.
Someday this rhyme,
Won't have you in it.

The Mix

Juice drops from a twisted root, into a bowl of clay,
Lands upon a cactus bloom and leaves of desert sage.
Then its gently ground up, with bone from a grizzly bear,
Made into a paste, for someone in despair.

Then it's smudged in smoke, to remove the evil spirits,
Medicine man he listens and only he can hear it.
With the evil spirits gone, his paste is pure again,
It's ready for some healing spirits, he gently stirs them in.

Now his paste is ready, to put it to the test,
He walks into a teepee, where a young girl rest.
She's wrapped up in a buffalo hide, cold as she could be,
Her hair is very wet, just sweating from her disease.

The medicine man he kneels, beside the sickened girl,
The smoke he smudges on her, slowly makes some swirls.
Then he takes the bowl, which has the healing mix,
And gently scoops some out, with short but holy sticks.

He places it on her forehead and also on her chest,
While others watched upon, just hoping for the best.
The medicine man he mumbles, words not known to them,
While reaching for the heavens, calling out the sin.

Then rising to his feet, he backs on out the door,
Now It's up to her, because he could do no more.
The sun was quickly setting, the girl she quietly rests,
And everyone in the tribe, was hoping for the best.

Then as the sun was rising, the girl came walking out,
Her fever it had broken, everyone began to shout.
The medicine man had healed her, she wore a happy grin,
On blended knee she thanked him and hugged her medicine friend.

What Hair

Sitting on the front row, with Elvis in my view,
Singing about a bald head, then I looked at you.
With a laughing crowd, I removed my hair,
Swaying with his music, I waved it in the air.

Elvis he was singing, "Are You lonesome tonight"?
My wife she started blushing, oh it was a sight.
I waved my hair while singing, you only live life once.
Even though they looked at me, as if I were a dunce.

23kachinas, thanks for the laugh my friend,
Times like these are priceless, I'll live them till the end.
It's more than just our money, that's in our bank account,
Enjoying life with humor, is what life's all about.

Thank You Forrest

Today I looked upon the blogs and got the saddened news,
Forrest has put some distance, away from me and you.
Even though we all will miss his words, I will respect his choice,
Thank you, Forrest for the "Chase" and the wisdom, in your voice.

You and Peggy enjoy your time, make the most of every day,
Go relax within your back yard and watch Tesuque play.
Forrest you have gave us, new adventures in our life,
Now enjoy your time with Peggy, your understanding wife.

I know I speak for all of us, each and every one,
Thanks for getting us off the couch, and out to smell the sun.
Thank you for the smiles, you placed upon our face,
Most of all thank you Forrest, for your amazing "Thrill of The Chase ".

My Herd

Sitting on my front porch, in my rocking chair,
Looking for my only cow, I know she's there somewhere.
My eyes they sweep my pasture, a small one acre wide,
How can a cow that big, find a place to hide?

Then I finally see my her, across my neighbors' fence,
She must have found the hole, the one I didn't mend.
I guess I'll go and get her and bring her back to home,
And put her on my acre ranch, so she can graze and roam.

My fence is newly mended, my cow is back home.
My neighbor he is happy, that now my cow is now gone.
With her on my acre, my mind starts to flow,
While drawing up my wife's new plans, for our soft lit patio.

Patiently Waiting

I've searched and searched, but what do I know,
Is "warm waters halt", really cold waters flow?
And the home of brown, seems simple to me,
But why does the brown have a capital B?

I've heard "This is No place for the meek",
Or brave you must leave, to hear what I speak,
You say that the "end is ever drawing nigh",
Or just the beginning, within sight of my eyes?

What do you mean "No paddle up my creek"?
If I'm traveling down, for the treasures I seek.
My heavy loads are getting lighter and lighter,
I'm not giving up; cause I am a fighter.

WHAT? If I've been "wise", "Are you joking?" I shout,
Just when I thought that I figured it out,
I'm not the sharpest, tool in the shed,
My wisdom is micro, up there in my head.

So, I'll patiently sit here, and wait for a winner,
Maybe they'll call me and invite me to dinner.

Name Is Called

I faced life's greatest challenge, I returned to my home,
Just as the doctor ordered, I rest and did not roam.
While surfing on the internet, for what the future holds,
I ran across ole Forrest Fenn and the stories of his gold.

For adventure I was thirsty, his chase was just the cure,
As soon as I was well enough, I'd joined his chase for sure.
That was several years ago, seven to be exact,
I jumped in with both feet and never did look back.

The chase gave me a reason, for what my life beholds,
In search for something greater, than his fancy box of gold.
Many miles I've traveled, many faces I have met.
Each like a wood burned memory, that I never will forget,

Giving up is not an option, it's my life I'm searching for,
Each day when I find it, I starve for even more.
My thoughts are quite expressive, my poetry shared to all,
My words they sometimes stumble, but I promise they won't fall.

My doctor seven years ago, thought rest would do me best.
But I must disagree, the chase beats in my chest.
And if I never find That box of yellow stuff,
Then that's alright by me, my Fennories are enough.

The knowledge is my mountains, imagination is my streams,
Faith's in my sky above, my Hope lives deep in me.
The friendships are my bonus, this chase gives life to all,
And each one I will cherish, until my name is called.

Flutter-by

It's not the "butter", nor the "fly",
Nor its "flutter", while passing "by".
It's the freedom upon, its wings so bold,
It's calming peace, its colors hold.

Live your life, as this tiny friend,
Live in peace, upon your wind.
So, others who look, upon you sigh,
And notice as, you "flutter-by"

Life Quest

I've done it tired, and now I'm weak,
Searching' around for the treasures I seek.
So many miles I have traveled, on my golden life quest,
My fingers were crossed, I hoped for the best.

Just to come up, a little bit shy,
One more trip, I just got to try.
Thank you Forrest , I wish you the best,
For daring me to take, this awesome life quest.

Crimson Shower

Just sitting in the woodlands, no one for miles around,
Autumn leaves are falling and floating to the ground.
Crimson leaves are hanging there, one tree just holding on,
Saving all its beauty, though many leaves are gone.

This tree looks like a monument, its Crimson leaves are bright,
Boldly shining for me, just knowing I'm in sight.
These woodlands have a special sound, I listen close to them,
I hear the singing sound, of nature's lovely hymn.

Just sitting in the solitude, of this amazing place,
I gently crack a softened smile, across my pleasured face.
A single doe just passed me, not knowing I was there,
Focused she continued, as if to get somewhere.

As I leave the woodlands, at the Crimson tree I stopped,
I was Standing at its trunk, just looking at its top.
Then all at once it happened, there came a gust of wind,
Crimson leaves start falling, from each and every limb.

It appears that it waited, for me to come along,
Showered by its leaves, till most of them were gone.
While crunching through the leaves, across the woodland sod,
It was then I realized, I was strolling with my God.

A Haiku for Fathers

Just wanted to say,
To all the fathers out there,
Happy Father's Day!

Charge

I fell to the floor, and suddenly waken,
And hit my head, oh how it's aching.
But it brought back some memories, that must really count,
I jumped to my feet and ran to my mount.

With both feet in the stirrups, my sword is at hand,
Pointing it forward, as I shout my command.
Kicking my heels, let the charging commence,
I gallop away and jump the wood fence.

Jdiggins has told me, there's gold in them hills,
Along with excitement, and all kind of thrills.
Adventure is flowing, all through my veins,
I'm not slowing down, till I finish this game.

If you see me out riding, upon my white horse,
Don't try to lure me, I'm staying on course.
The treasure awaits me, it will sure quench my thirst,
That's if jdiggins, don't beat me there first.

But if that were to happen, and this game were to end,
Congrats I would say, to a good online friend.

Dark Foggy Cabin

While returning home, from an awfully long trip,
Way down in October, the air had a nip.
My eyes were heavy, from driving so long,
Miles of staring, just listening to songs.

The GPS shined, boldly there on my dash,
My gas gauge was showing, I needed more gas.
I see a road, seemed a short way around,
Where I'd get some gas, at a small country town.

I made the turn, down the small road I went,
Enjoying the warm air, that blew from my vents.
As the sun was setting, my headlights came on,
My sense of adventure soon would be gone.

This dark little road, with a blanket of fog,
I jerked to the right, barely missing a log.
In just a few miles, my car it just quit,
I ran out of gas, now scared, I do sit.

I crack my window, and in came some fog,
In the distant I hear, the faint bark of a dog.
There must be a house, in the woods nearby,
What should I do? Should I give it a try?

I can't just sit here, in the dark all alone,
I got to get me some gas, so I can go home.
I walked through the woods, wet, cold and dark,
Closing in on the dog, that had a mean bark.

I arrived at a cabin, way back in the woods,
My hands are now shaking, I knew that they would.
A small candle burns, in the window I see,
The dog quickly turns, now he's barking at me.

The cabin door opens, an old man steps out,
" Who's out there?" He started to shout.
He pointed his light, brightly shined in my face,
Standing there frozen, can't move from my space.

" Who are you?" and" Why are you here?"
In a deep roughened voice, that rang in my ears.
I forced out the words, through the lump in my neck,
" I ran out of gas"," About a mile back."

" Don't just stand there", he said with a grin,
" My cabin is warm", and invited me in.
He gave me some coffee, and loaned me his coat,
"Be right back", he said, while clearing his throat.

Soon he came back, with a shiny gas can,
He looked evil and mean, but he was a nice man.
We jumped in his truck, and traveled not far,
He poured in my gas, and he started my car.

His words I'll remember, for as long as I live,
In an old, wrinkled voice, advice he did give.
"Next time you're out driving, on Halloween night".
" Don't take a back road, that's dark with no light".

" There's dangers that live, out here in the dark".
" with eyes that glow, and wolves that don't bark".
" I see your young and I see that your dareful".
" But to live and grow old, you gotta be careful".

As I drive off, I thought, what just happened?
Thank God I met a nice man, at that dark foggy cabin.

Ancient Happiness

Crimson in a darkened sky, dark hues above the trees,
Night it rests upon me and calms the gentle breeze.
In the stillness of the night, the sounds to me are great,
A hoot owl's lonely call, just searching for his mate.

Occasionally the sound, of a distant whippoorwill,
Echoes in the night, it breaks the nighttime still.
I'm sitting on the ground, leaning against a tree,
The sounds of night around me, although I cannot see.

Sitting in the darkness, my mind it drifts away,
To another time and place, of a long past distant way.
The Indians of New Mexico, who lived within that place,
Their strong will you could see, in the wrinkles on their face.

To get their daily food, the hunters traveled wide,
Preparing blankets for winter, scraping buffalo hides.
Wood was carried on their backs, then tossed into a pile,
The children also helped because, it usually took a while.

Life out in the desert, was harsh and extremely hot,
But they did not complain, they were happy for what they've got.
The New Mexico desert Indians, were an incredibly special breed,
Maybe we should listen, to what their telling you and me.

Even though it's tough at times, it's not the final end,
Be strong just like our natives, who roamed this land back then.
I know you have it in you, just look and you will find,
Your inner strength inside you, now let your happiness shine.

The Crimson in the darkened sky, now has turned to black,
It's time for me to stand and start slowly heading back.
Your life is what you make it, don't waste your only one,
For when you find your happiness, your life has just begun.

Choices

I look into the future, gaze in my crystal ball,
Three doors I see before me, wide but not real tall.
Each a different color, a choice that I must make,
Once a color's opened, that door then I must take.

First door is painted red, like the desert setting sun,
Looks so warm and cozy, inviting me to come.
Second door is painted green, like the grass beneath my feet,
But is the path beyond the door, equally as sweet?

Third door is painted blue, like the mighty sky above,
But if I step inside this door, will I soar like all the doves?
My choice is not reversible, once my final choice is made,
Will I labor in the sun, or rest within the shade?

All three seem so inviting, only one door leads the way,
A choice I know that I must make because I cannot stay.
I bow my head and ask for help, don't know what I should do,
Should I choose the door of red, or the door of green or blue?

A Mind That Sought

A journey through, a mind that sought,
Destinations end but travels naught.
Bound by earthly, dreams desired,
A distant place so oft inspired.

Through visions of, the days gone past,
Sees peace within, the hourglass.
Till one day starts, a lonely flight,
On journeys new, through visions sight.

Beyond the realms, of earthly things,
Like birds upon, their mighty wings.
Bound by peace and fearing naught,
A journey through, a mind that sought.

The Encounter

In the spring of 1540, a brand-new day beholds,
Spaniards mount their horses, seeking cities made of gold.
They ride throughout the sagebrush, thick and vastly spanned,
Below the mighty mesas, flat tops throughout the land.

Day by day they travel, not knowing where they'll end,
Pushed by springtime's subtle but welcomed southern wind.
Along a creek for water, no map to lead the way,
Toughened by the land, with each new passing day.

Upon a rise they rested, to gaze and just admire,
Then up ahead they noticed, the smoke from nearby fires.
With caution rode on forward, some Voices could be heard,
Although not understanding, the local native words.

Spaniards drew their weapons, rode fast into the tribe,
Chaos followed quickly; small children ran to hide.
No shots were fired upon them, the moment settled down,
The Spaniards soon dismounted, stood firm upon the ground.

With dusty hands of gesture, a message to the tribe,
Children start emerging, from places which they hide.
A few days pass with tension, by every man involved,
Both Spaniards and the Natives and how this all evolved.

One morning when the sun, had cracked the Mesa top,
The Spaniards on their horses, rode off and didn't stop.
In peace the natives gaze, not knowing what beholds,
But glad the Spaniards left, searching cities made of gold.

Value

Strive only for your heart's desire,
Not gold and shiny things.
To have a heart that one admires,
Be like a bell that rings.

A sound that others often hear,
Success from inside out.
But live your life, withhold what's near,
Rather than flaunt about.

To let your heart, direct your way,
Be all that you can be.
Of such a heart, now ring and say,
Value a life that's free.

Stairway to Heaven

Each Year's a run, upon the stairs,
That reaches to the sky.
Step by step we travel where,
Until we say goodbye.

Up into the clouds of white,
As years go passing by.
Admiring all the sounds and sights,
Way up in the sky.

Upon the final landing,
Before the golden gates.
Angels softly singing,
Departed family waits.

The gates of gold they swing,
A light shine from within.
It's time to meet the king,
He calls to come on in.

A warmness in your heart,
For eternity you are given.
Because you took a stepping start,
On that stairway up to heaven.

Time's Echo

Time it has an echo, just listen now my friend,
The past will come alive, repeating now and then.
If we listen to its echo, we'll know what lays ahead,
Our future will be brighter, by what the past has said.

I sit here in this desert space and with my ears tuned in,
I hear the echoes loudly and how it was back then.
Apaches lined in numbers, across these desert sands,
To fight for Mother Earth, to save their native lands.

I also hear the sounds, on a beach in Normandy,
Its gunfire ravished wildly, near the bluff along the sea.
Echoes keep a coming, as I sit here all alone,
I hear the brave young voices, once here and now they're gone.

In a humid seaside jungle, in a place called Vietnam,
Time it took more soldiers, it echoes in this sand.
I look across this desert, with sweat upon my brow,
I think about the wars, the time, the place, the how.

If we listen to time's echo and hear what lays ahead,
We can stop this crazy cycle; no war is worth the dead.
We all can make a difference, by the choices that we make,
Let's muffle out time's echo and live for goodness sake.

Fly

We live our life, from day to day,
Make choices, in hurried rush.
A decision made, come what may,
Living like, a bird in bush.

By time we spread, our wings to try,
What courage we have found.
We leave the nest and start to fly,
Get wind and soar around.

We live our life, by choices made,
Make all your dreams come true.
A bird that lives, within the shade,
Life pays it back to you.

By flight your life, you will embrace,
What waits within the sky?
We all will soar, smile on our face,
Give life a chance and fly.

My Daughter

Through many joyful learning years,
Her knees got scrapped I wiped her tears,
Small table in her room for tea,
My feathered hat she pours for me.

In her teens I must confess,
She tried and put me through the test.
From prom night leaving her friend,
I knew that someday this would end.

I know my child here by my side,
Will someday spread her wings and fly.
The memories I'll keep throughout the years,
I'll look at them through salty tears.

We finally made that drive to town,
To help her find that perfect gown.
She glances over from the book,
I give a smile and an approving look.

I know that on her special day,
I'll proudly walk and give her away.
The tears I'll shed and so will she,
Just seeing the woman she's came to be.

Times like these are bittersweet,
She'll do just fine, on her own two feet.
And if you read these words my girl,
We love your dearly, go find your world.

Mindy's Grandpop

As long as there are, stars in the skies,
You'll always see your grandpops eyes.

Just take the time, to gaze at them.
And cherish those many, memories of him.

Time may seem cruel, but it means no harm,
Someday in time, you'll be back in his arms.

Lonely Dreams

Neath skies of black, I dreamt,
Stars they flicker up above.
Here in my one-man tent,
Just living what I love.

Awaken from my peaceful dreams,
I lie here looking out.
Through netting with no seams,
My mind it drifts about.

Many nights I've pitched,
My tent upon these grounds.
Heard movements in the sticks,
And other nighttime sounds.

But tonight, an eerie feeling,
There are no sounds at all.
No unknown sounds a squealing,
No lonely hoot owl call.

Thinking about the chase,
And the poem, line by line.
And where his special place,
Could stand the test of time.

The chest is out there too,
Like me it sits alone.
Waiting for me or you,
To proudly take it home.

I need to get some rest,
Daytime will be long.
My solve put to the test,
I hope that I'm not wrong.

I close my eyes and drift away,
In dreams I quickly fall.
Beneath the hue of Milky Way,
And a hoot owls lonely call.

My Perfect Solve

I've done it tired, I too am weak,
For Years I've read, the words that he speaks.
I've tried to make, some sense of it,
Then all at once, my solve it just fits.

I pack my bags, in ten minutes flat,
Grabbed my keys, and my Favorite ole hat.
Say goodbyes, then shoot out the door,
Going to get, his treasures galore.

Hours I drive, with glorious thoughts,
Thinking of all, the treasures I've got.
I finally arrive, after driving all night,
I Sleep in my truck, just waiting on light.

The sun comes up, at the trail head I start,
I walk down the trail; I'm feeling real smart.
I get to my spot, can't believe what I see,
Others are there, just looking like me.

A couple was sitting, atop of my blaze,
Taking some selfies, with smiles on their face.
I held my composure, while cutting my eyes,
I Looked high and low, for one gracious prize.

Returned to my truck, no treasure in hand,
Feeling defeat, my solve was so grand.
Many hours I drive, just thinking a lot,
Word by word, the nine clues that I've got.

I pull in my drive, after driving all day,
Plop on my couch, now what can I say?
I've done it tired, I too am weak,
Still scratching my head, at the words he speaks.

Ancient Gift

The sky is Grey and gloomy, a chilly north wind blows,
I'm staring at the mountains, white capped from the snows.
Alone I sit in solitude, upon a Mesa top,
Sitting on a bear hide, across a flattened rock.

The year is 1540, I'm Navajo by birth,
While sitting I examine, my heart for what it's worth.
Below the smoke it rises, from fires within our tribe,
Blending with the gloomy sky, my gift now I must hide.

In my hand I hold, a fetish made by me,
Maybe in a thousand years, other eyes can see.
My gift is for the future, it's polished by my hands,
I'll leave it here beside me, here in my native lands.

I find a sheltered crevice, I place my gift inside,
I look up to the heavens, with my hands held high.
In my native tongue I speak, up to the mighty spirit,
In my heart I know, up in the clouds he hears it.

When my gift is found, they will hold it in their hands,
They will feel its ancient power, right here where I stand.
My gift will bring them solitude, they'll feel it in their heart,
Their life will have new meaning, while journeys they embark.

I softly say goodbye, it's for the future now,
I raise up to my feet, then notice parting clouds.
Sunray shines between them, lighting where I stand,
Approving rays from heaven, shine on for future man.

In my heart I know, I'll please a future soul,
It is time for me to leave now; time for me to go.
My heart is more than proud, upon this Mesa cliff,
Just knowing in future, they'll find my ancient gift.

Contentment

Your happy with your inner self and the life you live,
You don't care about the getting, all you want to do is give.
Your happy with your solitude and the feeling that it brings,
No need for fancy cars, or bright and shiny things.

If you only had one day to live, you would not sit down and grieve,
You would live it happy, just smiling as you leave.
Knowing that your family, know you've done your part,
They know while you are leaving, you're smiling in your heart.

Some they barely get by and some they strut their worth,
But those who find contentment, are the richest here on earth.
Me I found contentment, it's deep within my soul,
23kachinas I would also, like soup in a bread bowl.

Down the Line

The days are creeping closer, must faster now it seems,
A birthday for my soul mate, no longer in her teens.
Though years have caught up to her, she has that special shine,
What gift should I present her, I have one thing in mind.

Many, many years ago, we sat upon a beach,
Gazing at the children, all we could see was feet.
They were diving to the bottom, collecting tiny beads,
Sunken then for many years, beneath the waving sea.

I have them now before me, their colors bright and bold,
I wish they'd tell their secrets; I know they surely hold.
A necklace I will make, from beads with colors grand,
A birthday gift for her, to place within her hands.

One by one I slide, the beads along the string,
Thinking of the memories and all the things we've seen.
I hold a finished necklace, it's beauty bright and bold,
No gift can ever match it, our lifelong memories told.

Her special day arrives, her 89th grand year,
I gift to her the necklace; her smile gives way to tears.
Reminded of the memories, of a beach so far away,
Her silence is then broken, "I don't know what to say".

Two arms around my neck, her lips upon cheek,
Caught up in the moment, I too could hardly speak.
Her special day was perfect, thanks to our tiny beads,
Around her neck she wears them, so all the world can see.

She looks into my eyes, in her softened voice she speaks,
Wiping tears of joy, that's rolling Down her cheeks.
"I know my years are few and our granddaughter trails behind",
"I know she'll love this necklace, when I pass it down the line".

Eagles Claw

Spirits of the west, they whisper in the wind,
Softly in their speaking, stories of way back then.
Some spirits come in numbers, some spirits all alone,
Some arrive with visions, with pictures of their home.

While walking along a creek side, I was looking down,
I see a sharpened spear point, just lying on the ground.
I knelt there by the spear point, I was reaching with my hand,
The winds began just blowing, picking up the sand.

Just before I found it, the sky above was blue,
Darkness now upon me, no sun is shining through.
I tuck my face inside my shirt, to cover up my eyes,
That is when I heard him, much to my surprise.

A warrior spirit spoke to me, there in the blowing sand,
Says his name was Eagle Claw, a warrior for their clan.
He tells me that the spear point, once belonged to him,
And how he gently flaked it, to make it sharp and thin.

He tells his story to me, while sands still wildly blow,
He was walking along that creek side, many years ago.
He was faced up with a grizzly and with his spear in hand,
The bear began to charge him, there in that creek side sand.

Very tight he held his spear, the bear on hind legs stood,
He charged the bear and tried, to kill it if he could.
When the fight was over, the grizzly walked away,
Eagle Claw's days were over, his spirit flew away.

His spirit tells me take the point, it now belongs to me,
Then the winds they calm, sun bright as it can be.
I reach down to the spear point; I hold it in my hand.
Forever I will cherish, the skills within this man.

Then I leave the creek side, amazed at what I saw,
With my perfect spear point, made by Eagles Claw.

First

Walk into a forest, be first to stand that ground,
First person to see the sights from there, first to hear the sounds.
First to sit upon your log, first to see that flower,
While it's proudly shining there, in its finest hour.

First to see the chipmunks work, scurrying all about,
Carrying twigs into a hole, then quickly running out.
Be the first to look around, this this amazing piece of ground,
First to hear the eagles call, that breaks the silent sound.

First to see this babbling brook, reflecting light of day,
Heading for some lower ground, as it gently flows away.
First to feel the blowing wind, as it passes by this place,
First to sit upon a log, with it steady in your face.

Before you leave the forest, and go about your way,
First Give thanks to "God" above, for the forest in which you play.
As you leave, this heavenly place, first listen to what I say,
Give thanks for all the little things, you've seen throughout your day.

Because of him you're sitting there, reading my every verse,
Put the credit, where credit is due, and always put "God" First!

Eerie Place

Staring across a dim lit room, thinking I am alone,
A witch soars past upon her broom, there and then she's gone.
This castle high upon the hill, an eerie feeling rest's,
Slowly I continue, my fears put to the test.

Before me a large grand staircase, its rails in cobwebs stand.
Atop I see a shadow, a very well-dressed man.
And with a blink he is gone, I just got to see,
Slowly up the staircase, that is creaking back at me.

Atop of that grand staircase, a hall that is long and dark,
Rooms on either side, a ghost begins to hark.
A breeze begins to blow, cold within my face,
The smell of must around me, this is an eerie place.

Free

Live your lifetime free,
Let all your burdens escape,
Dream now my friend, dream.

Friends Are Right There

I gazed into my crystal ball,
Nothing there, no friends at all.
Smoke it circles near the sides,
They have left, they've gone to hide.

I placed my ball, upon the shelf,
Walked to the kitchen, to feed myself.
I opened the door, and before my eyes,
My friends jumped up, and yelled surprise.

Jdiggins was holding, a cake in hand,
Room full of friends, oh how grand!
I never heard them, they were quiet as can be,
Waiting in silence, just for me.

One thing I've learned and with you I will share,
When your friends are away, they're always right there.

Mother Earth

The year was 1640, in a place the desert spans,
Nothing in the distant, across the arid land.
Ajei lived within it, a Navajo by birth,
She'd sit upon the Mesa and connect with Mother Earth.

The summer has been hotter and drier than the rest,
Her people needed water, to pass their arid test.
The children stopped their playing, cracks upon their lips,
All pots were dry and dusty, the wet one saved to sip.

Ajei knew their fate depended, on rainfall through the year,
The water they must have, to live another year.
Her hair was black and dirty, her deerskin robe was dry,
She knew she had to go and at least give it a try.

She climbed the mighty Mesa, she sat upon the top,
Hands held high she prayed, for any little drop.
Mother Earth she listened, to Ajei's every word,
Then out across the desert, thunder could be heard.

The sky it darkened slowly, the winds began to blow,
Her people stood there gazing, in camp far down below.
Raindrops started slowly, then quickly picked up pace,
Cheers and smiles were all, across her people's face.

Ajei knew there's more, beyond her earthly stay,
For how the rains had come, on that hot and arid day.
If Hope seems dim and lacking, take it for what is worth,
Please go up on your Mesa and speak to Mother Earth.

Solitude

A bee flies in an open meadow, touching flowers one by one,
A beaver swims across the lake, his waves they flicker in the sun.
Above I hear an eagle's wail, while soaring through the sky,
A deer with her spotted fawn, then quickly caught my eye.

I sit upon a fallen tree, to give myself a rest,
I see a bluebird feeding, her babies in her nest.
While reaching in my backpack, to grab my sack of lunch,
A chipmunk stopped and stared at me, as if he had a hunch.

I pinched a piece bread, he acts as if he knew,
I took a bite of mine and said" here's a pinch for you".
Then across the lake I noticed, a darkness in the grass,
A moose was bedded down, beside it lay her calf.

Lunch is gone it's time to go and head back to my truck,
Then I heard them coming, at least a hundred ducks.
They landed on the water, no care that I was there,
The beaver turned and swam, as if to give his share.

With my pack it's time, to leave this heavenly place,
Away I walked while looking back, a smile was on my face.
Nothing like a lonely hike, across this mountain sod,
I'll take that back I wasn't alone; I was strolling with my God.

My Hero

Kentucky is a special place, it's where his life began,
In 1942, was born a special man.
Kentucky's full of horses, champions of all kinds,
But none can match the strength, of a boxer on my mind.

For 32 years he fought, his longest fight in life,
Parkinson's couldn't win, no matter how it tried.
He was the greatest man, to enter through the ropes,
Many tried to beat him, they left with diminished hopes.

He'll always be my hero, he was a man of faith,
I close my eyes and I can see, gold around his waist.
He danced around the ring, with a light as feather bounce,
Just waiting for the bell, so he could go and pounce.

Now his days are over, he left us with our dreams,
He was the greatest fighter; this world has ever seen.
Now he's up in heaven, gathering with old friends,
Though his days are over, his eternity just began.

Muhammad we will miss you, you've much enriched our lives,
Now it's you and God, to float throughout the skies.
Someday I will join you, up in that mighty place,
Someday I will thank you, I'll do it face to face.

A phrase you've always said, throughout the many years,
Forever it will ring, within our thankful ears.
"Float like a butterfly, sting like a bee",
This worlds going to miss you, see ya Muhammad Ali.

Remember

Remember our fallen soldiers, that fell throughout the years,
Remember the lonely families, who shed a million tears.
Remember the special hearts, that beat red, white and blue,
Remember those brave soldiers, that died for me and you.

Remember WWI, in tanks they fought with pride,
Remember WWII, on D-Day how they died.
Remember in Pearl Harbor, when the planes came soaring in,
Remember in Korea, they stopped the north again.

Remember Vietnam, in the jungles mighty thick,
Remember our brave soldiers, agent orange made them sick.
Remember those who fought and died over in Kuwait,
Remember Iraq and Afghanistan when our soldiers met their fate.

Remember the other skirmishes, all around this earth,
Remember our brave soldiers, who proudly showed their worth.
Remember the pride within them, how they died for you and me,
Remember the song that says, from sea to shining sea.

Remember today's for them, our soldiers that paid the price,
Remember to pause and thank them, for the freedom in your lives.
Remember in your prayers, those they left behind,
Remember freedoms cost, please keep it in your mind.

Remember as I salute you, from Generals to Cadets,
Forever I'll remember, I promise I'll never forget.

Spirit Lily

In the woods I walk alone, this trail is hard to see,
Years of growth have taken over, from the nearby trees.
I know this path leads somewhere, I just got to know,
Now on my knees and crawling, careful as I go.

I made it through the thicket, the thorns have brushed my arms,
Just a few small scratches, they're really no big harm.
Then I reach a clearing, and stand up to my feet,
Oh, the sight before me, everyone should see.

The sky above was cobalt blue, there's a warm and gentle breeze,
The water was free falling, from high above the trees.
This was the largest waterfall, I've seen throughout my days,
All I could do was stand there, with a fixed and steady gaze.

Just standing there in awe, such an amazing sight to see,
How the water falls forever, before it splashes by the trees.
I had to get a closer look, so I walked across the clearing,
Standing at the water's edge, now voices I start hearing.

I quickly turn around, I was startled as can be,
The clearing it was empty, no one there but me.
I noticed how the breeze, was cooler than before,
Then I heard that voice again, calling out once more.

" Don't be scared, I mean no harm", "they call me Running Deer",
" A hunter for our Indian tribe, I'm glad to have you here".
With open ears I listened, as his spirit talked to me,
He also had a vision, oh what a sight to see.

He was kneeling by the water's edge, a goose strung on his back,
Reaching for a water Lily, so he could take it back.
Peace was all around him and he as all alone,
With a Lillie for his wife, he quietly headed home.

Then the vision disappeared, his voice was soft and low,
His spirit slowly faded away, again the warm wind blows.
I looked up to the waterfall, swore no one I'd tell,
About the hunter spirit, that visited me on that trail.

If your ever in the woods and see a trail that's dim,
Who knows what you'll find, waiting at the end?
As I leave the waterfall, I feel the warmth within,
Because of ancient spirits, that visited in the wind.

Old Oak Tree

There comes a time, when all things must end,
Leaves begin falling, from an old oak tree.
Never to re-bloom, when the springtime begins,
No autumn colors, bright shining to see.

Standing there fragile, though once it was sound,
Strong winds they shake, it's limbs all about.
They crack and pop, then fall to the ground,
The lonely old oak is on its way out.

Soon there will be nothing, a stump where it stands,
No display of colors, softly waving about.
The bark is all falling, it's turning to sands,
Once the oak tree, was healthy and stout.

My memories of an oak that once stood,
Will always bring, a smile to my face.
Beautiful, bold, my memories in wood,
Grand as the new Sprig, that grows in its place.

Slow Rewards

To live a life in hurried stride,
In frantic pace and speed.
You miss the special things that hide,
Awaiting there indeed.

Like dew drops on a flower,
That rests in morning sun.
There in its finest hour,
As mornings just begun.

A rainbow in the distant,
The beauty of a storm.
It's colors in that instant,
Not in your daily norms.

Slow down and take moment,
To see what nature shows.
Enjoy the time, just own it,
As slowly on you go.

The Hunt

A hundred buffalo grazing, midst of an open plain,
Dark cloud in the distant, drops its precious rain.
Crawling in the grasses, while moving very slow,
A hunter for the Crow tribe, and in his hand his bow.

The wind is in his favor, the sun is at his back,
As he tops a gentle rise, all he could see was black.
He looks up to the heavens, but only with his eyes,
Prays his mighty arrow, would pierce a big bull's side.

So, he could feed his family, cold weeks that lay ahead.
And fur to cover his children, while lying in their bed.
He signals to another hunter, but never says a word,
One large bull has strayed away, from the moving herd.

He slowly takes an arrow and places on his string,
Gently raises to his knees and let's his arrow fling.
The arrow it flew straight and on a deadly path,
The bull had seen it coming and dodged its bloody wrath.

The herd it took off running, they shook the hollow ground,
The hunter hung his painted face, he let his family down.
But he will keep on hunting, the sun is still up high,
Maybe in a distant valley, he'll get another try.

He must continue hunting, his family depends on him,
So, they can eat and stay warm, during the winter winds.
Maybe you should listen, to the hunters of the past,
Just because you fail sometimes, don't give up so fast.

For if you keep on trying and continue to believe,
Someday you will gladly say," my goal has been achieved".

Time in Thought

Time in thought costs nothing,
Imaginations price is free.
Use them to your advantage,
Oh, the glorious sights you'll see.

Thank You Sir

Santa Fe awarded Forrest Fenn, with a city's proclamation,
Thanking him for" The Thrill of The Chase" and awaking a sleeping nation.
Many searchers pass through this town, while on their golden quest,
Looking for some treasures galore, hidden in an old-world chest.

If you have not taken the time to stop, while looking for a place to roam,
Stop and visit this beautiful place, that Forrest and Peggy call home.
Memories are created there, they'll last your whole life long,
The people, art and culture together sing a spiritual song.

Forrest you have created memories, by awaking a sleeping nation,
" Thank You Forrest" from all of us, on your Santa Fe proclamation.

Those

Struggles are among us, like chapters in a book,
Those who need a caring hand, just notice as you look.
Show the world your someone, not passing by in life,
Vow to make a difference, by helping those in strife.

Those standing on a corner, with their cardboard sign,
Wanting food or work, just trying to survive.
Those in a lonely alley, with needles in their arm,
Self-medicating drugs, that do their body harm.

Those who live in shanty shacks, no water in their home,
Living day by day, on gardens they have grown.
Those who live in hunger, so their children can live on,
Stretching every meal, until the last is gone.

Those deep in depression, curled up on their beds,
Fighting all the demons, that bounce within their heads.
Those in their cardboard box, on the streets that they call home,
On freezing winter nights, chilled down to the bone.

Those children who are orphans, no parents to guide their way,
Behind a chain link fence when they go outside to play.
Those within marriage, with bruises on their face,
Trying to get the nerve, to leave that painful place.

These are just a few, in this earthly home we're in,
Please take the time to care and help your fellow man.
We all can make a difference, but first we got to start,
Just lend a helping hand, you'll feel it in your heart.

Within My Hands

I walk into the desert, the smell of smoke is near,
I hear some voices calling, so gently on my ears.
I turn and look behind me, just me, I'm all alone,
The past is speaking to me, from others who are gone.

The sky above is cloudy, a breeze it gently blows,
The smell of nearby rain, so subtle on my nose.
I look up to a Mesa, brown and standing tall,
I hear their voices louder, the ancients as they call.

They welcomed me among them, into their native home,
A place that they had lived, before they died and gone.
One voice it calls me over, to nearby fallen stones,
She says that it's the place, her people called their home.

An overhanging ledge, with rooms built there below,
In awe I stand there gazing, my amazement surly showed.
I see an ancient fire pit, I smell the ancient ash,
I see some broken pottery, just laying where they smashed.

That is when I see it, sitting proudly by a wall,
A perfect pot with markings, no Cracks on it at all.
The ancient voice then tells me, to take her cherished pot,
Made by her own hands, with clay she went and got.

She says to show the world, that yes, she once was here,
Then she softly faded, her voice fell from my ears.
And with her pot in hand, I leave past nearby stones,
I promised Her I'd share, the stories of her home.

A gentle rain starts falling, the breeze still softly blows,
My ancient friend had gone, like me it's time to go.
The desert holds her secrets, her life here in the sand,
Me I hold her craftsmanship, her gift within my hands.

Youthful Hearts

Some live their life, staying young at heart,
But how is that possible? where do I start?
I've tried and tried, but to no avail,
The older I get, the less wind in my sail.

I've known others, whose spirits they soar,
Creeping on 80, with youthful galore.
Laughing and joking, as young, minded do,
No care in the world and joking with you.

I've got to find, the freedom they wear,
Youthful and glowing, without any care.
My heart grows eager, though it's growing old,
I'm not giving up, till it's youthful and bold.

Then I too can live the life of the young,
Then when I speak, youth roll off my tongue.
Age is a battle, that's not going to win,
I'm not laying down, I'm not giving in.

I will fight it for sure, with every beat of my heart,
Starting right now, with a new youthful start.

Spirit Bear

The year is 1530, I'm hunting for a bear,
Leaves are turning colors; chill is in the air.
While climbing up the mountain, I reach a rocky bluff,
I can't go any farther, my legs have had enough.

I rest upon a fallen tree, I'm looking all around,
Then all at once I heard it, a faint but grunting sound.
I raise up to my feet, I listen very well,
It came from out the bluff, as far as I could tell.

I walked along the rocks, while listening to that sound,
With my spear in hand, I was often looking down.
Then I reached a cave, a hole within the bluff,
As I slowly entered, I hear a softened gruff.

While holding back my spear, the bear came walking out,
All I could do is stare, he was very big and stout.
He was the largest bear, that I have ever seen,
When he looked at me, his eyes looked very mean.

Frozen in my tracks, we stared both eye to eye,
I couldn't throw my spear; I really don't know why.
The food I really needed, his fur would keep me warm,
But somehow, he just knew, That I would do no harm.

Then he walked away, he never did look back,
His back was lined in Grey, his body brownish black.
All at once I heard a voice, a spirit from long ago,
He said the bear had died, it's time for him to go.

Then the spirit tells me, to look within the cave,
As I look inside, there the huge bear laid.
In disbelief I turn around, a chill is in the air,
I knew I've seen the spirit, of that mighty, mighty bear.

Lost Memories

While sands fall through the hourglass and rest upon a mount,
I drift away to years gone past, more memories I recount.
Some memories live forever, others lost within the mix,
Today my memory's focused, on a memory with no fix.

Alzheimer's has a way, of stealing away the past,
A disease that's unforgiving, an evil without a mask.
This evil it has rested, on a loved one close to me,
Her memory it has faded, not like it used to be.

I remember the times she traveled, alone inside her car,
To visit us on the holidays, though didn't travel far.
When she knocked upon our door, greetings she always said,
She always wore a smile, while holding banana nut bread.

My memory it is vivid, though hers is fading fast,
She has no recollection, of her childhood or her past.
My memory I would give her, in a second if I could,
All of us could make a difference, that is if we would.

There are people all across this land, in Alzheimer's evil grasp,
Their memory gone forever, living without their past.
Many work within their labs, attacking this dreaded disease,
Find a box and donate a dollar and help them, would you please?

My Masterpiece

Standing in the wilderness, my easel in front of me,
Looking at a waterfall, flowing majestically.
With oils upon my palette, my brush within my hand,
I'll try to paint the moment, of this solitude so grand.

My canvas white at blank, I dip my favorite brush,
With gentle strokes I paint, the waters as they rush.
I paint upon my canvas, the rocks so mighty high,
Water falling boldly, beneath a pale blue sky.

I carefully continue, to paint this solemn place,
Me I continue painting, with a smile upon my face.
I hear the rushing water, of this mighty waterfall,
I see my finished painting; I've painted here for all.

I gather up my oils and clean my brushes good,
Pack up my trusty easel, out here in the woods.
I look up to the waterfall, one last and final time,
I turn and walk away, beneath the warm sunshine.

To me this place is magic, I feel it deep within,
Captured on my canvas, like a writer with his pen.
The breeze is warm and gentle, blowing through the trees,
And me I hope the world, enjoys my masterpiece.

Life's Aromas

Time is like a fragrance, it quickly drifts away,
Pleasing in the moment, then gone by passing days.
Stop and smell the roses and the aromas that they give,
Cherish a life of fragrance and all that it can give.

Springtime Flowers blooming, with each a scent their own,
Like deep within a forest, where many pines have grown.
Summer rains beginning, upon a dusty road,
The freshness on a mountain, covered in white snow.

Time will slow its frantic pace, its fragrance in the wind,
Just for you to cherish it, from beginning to the end.
Time is here and then it's gone, like scent it softly goes,
Use it very wisely and breath from just your nose.

Birthday Wishes

Hello jdiggins, just thought I would drop in,
Just to say hi to you, my real good online friend.
Keep having your fun, till the angels they come,
Kick up your heels and reach for the sun.

Enjoy the things you do on the way,
You will never look back, and regret it someday,
Wishing you a life, happy and true,
Oh! I almost forgot HAPPY BIRTHDAY to you!

Cherish the Moments

While chasing your dreams,
Cherish the moments my friend,
Life is much too short.

Final Prize

To live is to love, your inner self,
Find your happiness, not the wealth.
True journeys now, you must start,
Peace awaits, within your heart.

You won't regret, your peaceful trip,
Must you take, your inner step.
First look around, the world you live,
Search not for take, search now for give.

Your journeys here, now go embark,
Soul ignites, your special spark.
For if you search, with not your eyes,
Happiness awaits, your final prize.

Broken Silence

Raindrops down the windowpane, a distant thunder heard,
Beside my fire aglow, in silence not a word.
Gazing in my fireplace, at dancing tiny flames,
Alone here in my thoughts, about life they quickly came.

No, I am not a singer, nor painter with his art,
I am not a CEO, in a high-rise touching stars.
Yet I am not a beggar, or homeless on the street,
Holding out my hands, to everyone I meet.

I am somewhere in the middle, I am happy living here,
Life's not about the fortunes, or kind of car I steer.
Our daily lives hold treasures, but first you must look,
Smiles from a total stranger, or stories from a book.

A cozy little fire, like this I sit besides,
Raindrops on the window, or the thunder heard outside.
The treasures they are endless, for those who truly live,
It is not about the getting, it is more about what you give.

Two coffee cups beside me, steam rising from their tops,
I smile while looking over, at the treasures that I've got.
My fire is burning low now, the rain outside has end,
The silence is then broken, awakes my homeless friend.

Go Get It

The pirates they drift, the same waters as you,
With vessels so heavy, with gold bullion's too.
They stash it on islands, bury it deep,
To someday return, their treasures to keep.

But they do not know, you are drifting about,
Upon finding their loot, you will carry it out.
Jdiggins start fanning, that hanging ole sail,
And show them darn pirates, that you will prevail.

Snatch all their loot, and make you some wind,
I am cheering you onward, go get it my friend!

Forever Will Stay

May the waters for you, eternity flow,
Onward in journeys, you may yet to know.
Life's meandering brook, may ripple astray,
Your soul my friend, forever will stay.

Crimson

Another day has ended, how time it seems to fly,
My feet are hanging off the dock, beneath a crimson sky.
There are no winds a blowing, the water looks like glass,
Time is like a sunset; it moves extremely fast.

The sun is barely hanging there, it's round as it can be,
It's reflection on the water, it bounces up at me.
The lake it looks like Crimson, just like the evening sky,
A perfect time to ponder and ask the question why.

Why would any man, just throw this all away?
And give his life for me, so he could light the way.
Feet hanging off the dock, I search inside my heart,
Looking for the answers, to why he done his part.

The sun is getting lower, it's falling from the sky,
Then I feel the answer, to my question why.
It's not about the days, I walk upon this earth,
It's not about fancy cars, or my banking worth.

It's about my inner self, the happy life I live,
A gift direct from him, which he chose to give.
When my days are over, now at least I know,
Sunsets will last forever; I'll have a place to go.

I raise up to my feet, right there where I stood,
And thanked him for his gift, wrapped in his Crimson blood.

For the Record

The ins and outs, the ups and downs,
This chase has given us, smiles and frowns.
From hot to cold, from brave to meek,
In search of one small thing, we seek.

We push and pull, most every rock,
In hopes to find, that waiting shock.
Not dumb nor wise, stuck in the middle,
If we could only, solve this riddle.

But why so quickly, when slows our pace,
Must We be fast, to win this race?
Surely not, we doubt and pray,
If that's the case, we'll need Ben-Gay.

We've walked with lights, in dark of night,
We've climbed the hills, from low to high.
In search for the elusive blaze,
Somewhere north, of Santa Fe.

Together we go, alone in there,
As one we make, a perfect pair.
Trek on my friends, through sun and rain,
And for the record, we're not insane.

The Christmas Carol

While sitting on the sofa, my doorbell began to ring,
Walking to my front door, I then could hear them sing.
Before I opened up the door, I knew what I would see,
People dressed in festive clothes, singing just for me.

When I pulled the door Aside, they were standing in a row,
Singing Silent Night for me, their faces how the glowed.
Each person singing proudly, standing straight and tall,
While listening to their singing words, the snow began to fall.

It didn't seem to faze them, each person singing proud,
Just for me and me alone, as if I were a crowd.
While they stood there singing, I looked up in the sky,
Snowflakes landing on my face, oh what a holy night.

When the song was finished, they turned and walked away,
Left me standing there alone, there in my cold doorway.
Thinking about this time of year and what it really meant,
My minds awaken by the sounds, of the angels God has sent.

Born within a stable, they came from miles around,
To see the mighty holy king and hear his holy sound.
Please don't sit upon on your sofa, waiting for your bell to ring.
Go and show your thanks to God, this Christmas go and sing.

I just opened a gift from him, he gave me years ago,
All because of Silent Night, they sang there in the snow.
My heart is full of Christmas past, just busting at the seams,
I think I'll walk on down the street and help them as they sing.

Merry Christmas everyone, my friends from shore to shore,
Listen close, you might just hear, me singing outside your door.

Snowy Christmas Eve Night

While looking in the darkness,
Mamas thoughts they run astray,
Papa said that he'd return,
In just a couple days.

A week has passed since leaving,
For the food they dearly need.
The howling wind it carries,
The snow on past the trees.

Their fire it slowly flickers,
Only three sticks left to use,
Burn them now or morning?
Which one, she now must choose.

Their Christmas Eve's been harder,
Than any year before.
Mamma she then heard it,
Boots stomping at the door.

Their wooden door swung open,
The snow it drifted in.
There stood the kiddos papa,
All bound up with a grin.

An armload full of wood,
A sack tied to his belt.
For sure, the greatest Christmas,
That mama ever felt.

For she received her present,
Oh, such a welcomed sight,
Removed his coat and hugged him,
On a snowy Christmas Eve night.

Strawshadow

When you're feeling shaded and your days not going right.
Walk into a meadow, where the shade is out of sight.
As your standing there, your shadows there again.
Together you'll feel better, trust me I'm your friend.

The Special One

The holy Grail of Santa Fe, sits silent in repose,
For a day or a thousand years, no one really knows.
Waiting for a special one, whom many hours spent,
Trying to decode a poem, that one ole man has sent.

For when they proudly lay their eyes, upon that golden place,
Let's not forget ole Forrest Fenn, who gave us this golden race.
Without him we would be living, our normal everyday lives,
Not living out adventure, searching for his gracious prize.

A selfless act, by a selfless man, just for you and me.
Should forever be written with pen of gold, in the book of history.
So, ask yourself, if had the means, could you have done it too?
If not, then a thing called greed, lives deep inside of you.

So, while you're on adventure, looking for That Holy Grail,
Take the time to thank the man, who put wind within your sail!

Scales of Joy

Deep within my eyes of scale,
A Heartbeat can be heard.
For all who have traveled past the vale,
Sounds out it's every word.

An empty void, of eternal days,
Scales of my heart deploy.
No pain or hurt can wipe away,
My pooling scales of joy.

Specialklr's Trip

Talent is under rated, imagination takes you far,
To places out of reach, in your everyday family car.
Take a trip Specialklr and leave your car behind,
You too have words within you, look and you will find.

When your trip is over, with your feet back on the earth.
You will see imagination, truly has its worth.
Talent it is handy, imagination never ends,
Now tell us of your trip Specialklr, except tell us with your pen.

Without the Fear

Why is it birds fly around?
Yet I must stroll upon the ground.
And cheetahs run, so fast and strong,
But weakly I move slow along.

The owl it sees within the night,
Yet then again it blinds my sight.
And penguins swim in waters cold,
I'd surely die to be that bold.

I do not fly, run strong and fast,
Nor in the night, I see not past.
But there's one thing I surely know,
I need not these things down here below,

For when my final day has come,
Along the cheetah I plan to run.
Without the fear, through black of night,
With the birds I'll fly into the light.

Ramona's Bouquet

I'm awfully glad that you stopped by,
To drop a note to read.
Pull up a chair, I'll tell you why,
Here's where we plant our seeds.

We water them with friendship,
Until they start to grow.
Fertilize with Penmanship,
Then let our minds just flow.

Then our poems bloom,
Colors shining bright.
They brighten up the room,
each and every night.

Ramona stop again,
As your passing through,
What we have as friends,
Is a bouquet made just for you.

Wild & Free

As I hike through morning fog, my trail disappears in Grey,
As time moves on, it will lift and slowly rise away.
Then I will see much farther, down this narrow path I stroll,
But Until it does, I guess I'll sit, atop of this foggy knoll.

While sitting on the trail side, my mind it drifts away,
To a time when I was hiking, on a bright and sunny day.
Way up in the mountains, I was far from any town,
Walking along a cliff side, nervous and looking down.

I found the strength within myself, to stop there on that trail,
Admiring the beauty, of an eagle, while on the wind he sailed.
I remember when the eagle perched, upon an old dead tree.
Oh, the beauty in his stance, so proud, so wild, so free.

The freedom that I felt that day, while the eagle posed for me,
Nothing could really match it; I too was wild and free.
I could fly along these trails, no care where they might end,
Alone just wild and free, just as my feathered friend.

Freedom comes in many forms, each person has their own,
I found mine there on the trail, as I slowly roamed.
Then the fog starts rising, I'll soon be on my way,
I'll leave this knoll, just listen to what I say.

Free yourself and take the time, to walk a lonely trail,
Go and find your freedom and listen to feathered wails.
You will not be sorry, you'll have a heck of a day,
All the troubles you had in town; I promise will drift away.

Old Home Place

Sunlight beams, through leaves of gold,
Brisk in air, chilly and cold.
Remote I stand, near tales of old,
Silence here, no stories told.

Rocks that rise, unto the sky,
No smell of smoke, just lonely I.
Forest floor, with raging vine,
Taking over, through midst of time.

Vines to cover, the rocks of home,
Time did win, now all is gone.
Circle of rock, of old open well,
Bucket of rust decayed where it fell.

Silence it soothes, my heart as I roam,
At an old place, my ancestors called home.
Sun sets lower, with each passing minute,
Chill is much colder, but proud that I'm in it.

I leave with feeling, whole once again,
Replenished by family, ancestors of kin.
Before I leave, this place that I roam,
Thanks to my family, for calling me home.

The sun is now set, dark moving in fast,
Please take the time, to visit your past.
Your heart wont regret it, no not for a minute,
Let the past come alive, let family back in it.

In silent repose, your old home place waits,
For you to come visit, with smile on your face.
Dark is now here, a single owl hoot,
Replenish your soul, go visit your roots.

330   *James Bynum*

Spring

In the morning sun,
Frost upon a daffodil,
Springtime emerges.

My Apache Bandanna

Riding through the desert, alone upon my horse,
The breeze is slightly blowing, trying to stay on course.
On either side the mesa's, stand so very tall,
Above I see an eagle, I hear his lovely call.

The sun is high above me, the sky is clear and blue,
The colors of the mesa's add a reddish hue.
All day in the saddle, just seems to take its toll,
Then all at once I seen him, alone upon a knoll.

An Indian boy was sitting, not caring I was near,
I notice as I ride up, he's not showing any fear.
I climbed down from my saddle, with my reins in hand,
His face was chapped and red, just sitting in the sand.

I offered him some water, from my old canteen,
He began to drink, most thirst that I have seen.
Lost out in this desert, a boy would surely die,
I helped him on my horse, and we began to ride.

Not a word was spoken, he grabbed around my waist,
The sun was bearing down, upon this arid place.
For miles we ventured onward, daring not to stop,
Then I noticed something, upon the Mesa top.

It was a line of Indians, all mounted on their horse,
Slowly I continued, just staying on my course.
They look to be Apache, with bands around their head,
The Feathers on their spears, in the sun was vivid red.

Then single file they rode, down from the Mesa top,
I gently pulled my reins, my horse it gladly stopped.
We climbed down from my horse, my blood was pumping fast,
Together we just stood there, they were approaching fast.

About a hundred yards away, they stopped all in a line,
Standing behind the boy, I knew that it was time.
My hands upon his shoulders, we slowly walk to them,
The Indians start their chanting, each and every man.

The boy he finally speaks out, in his native tongue,
Suddenly the chanting stops, as quick as it begun.
Then a lone Apache, swings down from his horse,
Speaking as he walks up, his voice was harsh and course.

The Apache boy ran to him, and hugged him on the leg,
The Apache man then took, his bandanna from his head.
He held it out to give me, his thanks within his hand,
Gladly I accepted, then nodded to that man.

They climbed upon his horse, the chanting once again,
And then they rode away, in dust from desert sand.
Alone within this desert, on a nice and sunny day,
His bandanna around my neck, I slowly ride away.

Morning Light

The beautiful smell of sunshine,
And the sounds of dancing rays.
In silence echoes loudly,
Through the early morning haze.

Gleaming light on mountain tops,
With its valley shadows dim.
Deep within the forest,
A brand-new day begins.

No one to see its beauty,
No one to hear it's sounds.
No one to spoil the moment,
No one upon its grounds.

Its solitude it glistens,
Like dew drops on its floor.
Just waiting for a stranger,
To come visit and adore.

So, take a trail to nowhere,
Go well before it's light.
And You become that stranger,
And adore its morning light.

Our Flag

Our Flag
Many believe in it,
Many honor it.
Many respect it,
Many fly it.
Many test it.
Many live for it,
Many die for it.
Our Flag.

Proofread

Pdenver you are funny, you sure know how to yak,
I don't even worry; I know you've got my back.
When I am finished typing, and ready to hit the send,
It sure is comfort knowing that it's proofread by my friend.

My Shining Rose

The morning sun is rising, I'm finally here at last,
Standing at the gateway, to the garden of my past.
A rod iron gate before me, it's rusted now from time,
The rod iron fence that joins it, overtaken by the vines.

With a little effort, the gate I pushed aside,
And enter in the garden, but much to my surprise.
This garden of my past, once didn't have a weed,
Now they've taken over, it's very much in need.

A pathway is before me, created by some stones,
While walking I sure noticed, my gardens almost gone.
The roses that once flourished, with pink, yellow and red,
Now their thorny branches, are overgrown and dead.

I walk up to a tiny pond, I built it in my past,
Within it dirty water, it's still and looks like glass.
I kneel by the tiny pond, and lean to look within,
But in my sharp reflection I see, my face without a grin.

The years have caught up to me, with wrinkles on my face,
Soon just like the roses, I'll leave my garden space.
That is when I see it, midst everything that's dead,
One tiny little rose, just glowing pinkish red.

I clean out all around it and till the softened ground,
I could see within its color, it's proud that it was found.
As I leave my garden, one thought has come to mind,
I know my garden lives, even after all this time.

So, if you have a garden, a garden of your past,
Go and check it out because time moves very fast.
The sun has finally risen, it warms me as I go,
While leaving, one more final look, I see my shining rose.

Starry Skies

We are just a tiny speck, in the universe and stars,
Our life is just a moment, in the hourglass of Mars.
So, live your life with purpose, your moment as it flies,
And take some time to gaze, up in a nighttime sky.

A million stars await you and distant planets too,
In the nighttime starry sky, shining just for you.
But while your gazing upwards, take some time in thought,
About your life on earth and everything you've got.

Friends you have around you, like Saturn with its ring,
Your family shining for you, like shooting stars that fling.
Your moment is a notepad, you hold your pen to write,
Begin your words while looking, up in a starry night.

You only live life once, don't waste it passing by,
The answers you are needing, are in the nighttime sky.
The hourglass of Mars, will one day lose its sands,
Your moment will be over, you'll leave this earthly land.

There's more awaiting for you, beyond the distant stars,
And there will be no hourglass, in your universe afar.
So, grab your pen and write my friends, give an honest try,
So, when your moment passes, we'll meet in starry skies.

Thank You

Thanks to you all soldiers, across this beautiful land,
Who fought for our country, and for your fellow man.
Because of all your courage, and willing life to give,
Millions now have freedom, in this land that we live.

A soldier has a special heart, it beats red, white and blue,
Leaves his family alone at home, for the lives of me and you.
A soldier's courage will not fade, when dangers drawing nigh,
No matter what the outcome, a soldier's going to try.

It takes a very special breed, when duty calls their name,
Not looking for the glamor, not wanting any fame.
Many soldiers fought for freedom, many soldiers died,
Many soldiers carried brothers; many families cried.

I salute to you all soldiers, two fingers on my brow,
For those who fought unselfishly, the wars of then and now.
A challenge to all American's, who live across our lands,
Find a soldier, seek one out, and proudly shake their hand.

My Cherokee Frog

Standing at the trailhead, my gear strung on my back,
The sun is just now rising, its rays begin to crack.
The fog it softly lingers, a chill is in the air,
A dew rests on the forest floor, a sound of river near.

I begin my journey, just walking down the trail,
Like a boat upon the waters, I open up my sail.
There's nothing like the solitude, hiking all alone,
I'll spend my day enjoying, mother nature as I roam.

On the trail while walking, an Eagle's in the sky,
He softly floats along, while he's on the fly.
I wonder if he sees me, from way up in the air,
If he does, I doubt, that he even cares.

I hike along the river's edge, the water it quietly flows,
As if to sneak away, rippling as it flows.
Up ahead I see a pool, in the quickly fading fog,
Beside it stands a deer, drinking near a log.

I try to sneak up on it, I wondered if I could,
The deer just raised its head and bounced into the woods.
When I reached the pool, I gazed into the water,
While watching all the rainbows, I hear a rain crow holler.

Up ahead I see a rock, to pause and rest my feet,
That is where it happened, a spirit spoke to me.
His vision was before me, just floating in the air,
Me I was in awe, just quietly sitting there.

He said he walked this trail, many years ago,
He too enjoyed its beauty, he wanted me to know.
He said he was a Cherokee, he once lived up ahead,
Near a mighty waterfall, that is what he said.

He said he left me something, inside its misty fog,
He carved it from a stone, an ancient little frog.
Then his spirit disappeared, just faded in the air,
Up the trail I hurried, just trying to get there.

When I reached the waterfall, I knew that it was there,
Then I quickly entered, its mist within the air.
Behind that mighty waterfall, in a carved out tiny space,
Wet the frog was sitting there, a smile upon my face.

I took the ancient frog, and went back to the trail,
There I sat and starred at it, the stories it could tell.
The sun was getting lower, it's time to head on back,
Carefully I placed the frog, safe within my pack.

When I reached my pickup, I headed back to town,
I Couldn't wait to show, the ancient frog that I had found.

The Mirror

One looks into a mirror, to fix their daily hair.
But do they really see, the image really there?
Within the silvered glass, there hanging on the wall,
Your image stares back at you, as you would look to all.

There's much more to be seen, while you're standing there,
Much more than your image, or the color of your hair.
The mirror it reflects, a living, breathing soul,
That sure can make a difference, daily as you go.

Small deeds for those around you, a smile while passing by,
Can change the world with kindness, stop rockets in the sky.
A smile can be contagious, let's start an epidemic,
Your mirrored friend will glisten, just knowing you began it.

While gazing in the mirror, there's many things you'll see,
Be proud of your self-image, be proud of who you'll be.
Go now and make a difference and show the world you care,
But first, go thank the image, for the strength within its stare.

Ancient Promise

A soul along the water's edge,
Awaits what lies ahead.
The light within an ancient pledge,
A promise that was said.

Waves rock the soul, to and fro,
So gently on its stance.
Yearning for its time to go,
It soon will have its chance.

An eastern light appearing,
A promised tide it grows,
No longer its adhering,
And gently off it flows.

An ancient pledge was spoken,
An ancient promise kept.
An ancient soul then joined it,
And together, off they swept.

Desert Skies

Strangers came into our lands, their wealthy riches sought,
At all the cost of native man, we vowed to give them naught.
The stillness in the desert, was broke by pounding hoofs,
Gunshot rings would echo, from far Adobe roofs.

The blood that runs within me, each drop is filled with Pride,
For as long as it is flowing, I will not run and hide.
This vastness in the desert, the warmth within its winds,
The spirits that it carries, till death I will defend.

The strangers came in numbers, they swept across our land,
Hateful in their looting, to our women and our men.
Years they slowly passed, but I knew the time was near,
Alone the spirits found me and whispered in my ears.

In tiny ropes I tied, a knot for passing days,
And rode to all my neighbors, to each a rope I gave.
With each new morning sun, a knot would be untied,
When the knots have vanished, together we would rise.

The desert morning started, to us was no surprise,
I'll not forget the look, within the stranger's eyes.
We forced the strangers southward, they quickly fled our land,
The pride within the Navajo, filled each and every man.

When trouble finds you sleeping, remember this my friend,
You're not alone, there's many, who'll help you till the end.
And when your trouble leaves you and prides within your eyes,
Remember me the spirit, who lives in the desert skies.

Friendly Apple Pie

My pie is in the oven, my mind it drifts away,
About the apple pie I baked, just the other day.
I cut it up in slices, and proudly passed it out,
To friends who really wanted some, that's what it's all about.

Though the pie was small, and the slices they were thin,
Everyone enjoyed their slice, except for one good friend.
CindyM, I know you missed out, but glad to see ya back,
For you I have one whole pie, sitting on my baker's rack.

I've always been the honest type, and do the things I say,
So, Here's a pie just for you, just like the other day.
But there is one small difference, from the other pie I cooked,
The apples are not quite as fresh, and I didn't need a book.

I said that I would bake one, just for you my friend,
It's the thought that really counts, I'll serve it with a grin.
I didn't have fresh picked apples, please don't be mad at me,
The apple pie I cooked for you; it is a Sara Lee.

From Son to Father

Father I say, I'm not afraid,
I fear not the shadows that lurk in the shade.
For I am brave, and know you are here,
Because of this, I will not fear.

Father you've taught me all sorts of things,
I've listened to you, the joy that it brings.
Knowing someday, the angels will come,
And take you from me, on your journey home.

When that time comes and you must leave,
I will carry your words with me on my sleeve.
And cherish them always, as if you were here,
I'll try my best to hold back the tears.

Father you've made me, the man that I am,
A reflection of you, a very strong man.
Until the day, the angels arrive,
Let's just have fun, while we're feeling" ALIVE ".

Why

Beneath a mighty oak, I bask in summer shade,
Leaning against the trunk, on a early summer day.
Chewing on a twig, my knees they're raised up high,
Lost within my daydream, searching reasons why.

Why did Forrest give us, this journey we are on?
To get us off the couch. For trails to walk upon.
To fill our minds with knowledge. Learning as we go?
To watch us from afar. While imaginations grow?

A warm and steady breeze, blowing gently in my face,
Alone I sit and ponder, in the solitude of this place.
Together it has brought us, though many we are one,
While looking for his treasure, friendships have begun.

Is it for the stories? To tell us of his life.
His years of great adventures? With Peggy as his wife?
Is it for the hope, and dreams he gives to all?
So, we can have adventure? And hear an eagle's call.

The summer sun is falling, it's time for me to go,
Why he really done this, I may never know.
But as I walk away, beneath a golden sky,
Aloud to Forrest I thank him, for whatever reason Why.

To Catch A Shining Star

To fish upon a starry night,
Catch all the stars you can.
Your catch will be, just shining bright,
Dreams will fill your pan.

You fish within the darkened night,
Must take your precious time.
First spot your star, shining bright.
Cast out your fishing line.

Within the night, your bending pole,
A shiny star you took.
Starry in your fishing hole,
Night as you set your hook.

My Cottonwood

Many, many years ago, in a hidden valley floor,
Teepees stood in numbers, along a creek side shore.
The smoke it drifted gently, in the early morning breeze,
With golden tips of sunlight, atop the nearby trees.

While gazing down upon it, I noticed something near,
Across the creek below them, a pair of spotted deer.
Tiny in their stance, the two they jumped about,
While mama she was grazing, alert and looking out.

The sky above was scattered, with clouds all golden white,
Oh, what a peaceful morning, to look upon this sight.
My people start their moving, around the camp below,
Mama waves up to me, I know it's time to go.

Before I leave this beauty, there's something I must do,
I kneel beneath a cottonwood, remove my deerskin shoes.
Both hands upon its trunk, I gaze at limbs above,
I pray into the heavens; give thanks for things I love.

Like this lonely cottonwood, I too must have the sun,
Like it my roots grew slowly since my earthly life begun.
Someday I'll surely grow, just as big and strong,
I'll bask in morning sunshine; I'll help sing nature's song.

As I slowly stumble, down to our valley floor,
I know that more awaits me, beyond life's golden shore.
I hear my people speaking, I smell the burning wood,
I turn for one last look, at my heavenly cottonwood.

Turquoise Beads

Many, many years ago, some turquoise beads were found,
At an ancient pueblo, just scattered on the ground.
The Indians who lived in there, they called this place their home,
Who made the beads? Who took their time? that never will be known.

The beads were small, shaped like discs, with a perfect little hole,
Polished to perfection, crafted from their soul.
Looks as if they were made to string upon some twine,
To make a stunning necklace, for that date and time.

But who knows why they ended up, scattered across this ground so cold,
If only they could talk to us, the stories that would be told.
Why the Indians living there, they quickly up and run,
Was it cause of hunger? No food to feed their young.

22 beads were gathered there, Held in the finder's fist,
With visions of a bracelet, to wear upon his wrist,
All the beads were given, to an Indian with the skill,
To create a silver bracelet, with very much appeal.

The turquoise beads were polished, placed neatly in a row,
On a silver bracelet, to proudly let them show.
The bracelet it has been worn, on wrists of many men,
Then it finally ended up, on the wrist of Forrest Fenn.

Proudly Forrest wore them, those precious turquoise rocks,
Until one day, he took them off, and placed them in a box,
He hid the box and challenged us to find where it is hid,
Knowing a worthy person, will someday raise the lid.

No doubt this worthy person will have a smile upon their face,
To see the bracelet laying there, with all its poise and grace,
Forrest will be happy, to see his bracelet again,
Just to have it on his wrist, will surely make him grin.

And if a thousand years have passed, before someone finds the box,
Then they will place it on their wrist, and feel those powerful rocks,
One thing for sure, now or then, when that day's finally here,
If they Listen very closely, one proud Indian they will Hear.

Memories of Color

Time it swiftly moves, memories fade away,
Lost within our minds, covered by the Grey.
Memories that are spoken, brought up now and then,
Last a little longer and shapes a subtle grin.

She was a fellow searcher, some of you did know,
Even fighting cancer, she had a special glow.
She had a kindled spirit, you could see it in her smile,
If given just a half an inch, she'd stretch it for a mile.

Before the memories fade away, and Grey starts moving in,
Remember our fellow searcher, and how it was back then.
When many pulled together, on an incredibly special day,
To show her how we care and by her all the way.

Even though she's left us, I feel as if she's near,
Whispering words from heaven, listen and you'll hear.
Cheering on the searchers, while on their golden chase,
I know in heaven she wears, a smile upon her face.

I just replaced the Grey, with colors bright and bold,
Your memories of color, forever we shall hold.
Everyone who reads this, remember those who fell,
Most of all remember our friend we called "Renelle".

The Sweat Lodge

In the year of 1540, I lived upon this land,
Way out in a desert, with my noble clan.
One day while I as hunting, looking for some food,
The evil spirits found me and changed my happy mood.

I broke my bow in anger, no food I've killed that day,
I grabbed my knife of bone and also threw away.
I knelt down to my knees, I begged into the wind,
"Please take these evil thoughts, they'll kill me in the end".

I walked back to our village, others looked at me,
They knew that I was different, they prepared a place for me.
They called this place a sweat lodge, where evil is forced out,
Replaced by holy spirits, that's what it's all about.

The lodge was made of saplings, covered with some hide,
Red hot stones were placed, for heating the inside.
As I slowly walked past, where the skull was hung,
Chants were heard by others, speaking native tongue.

Then I passed the sacred fire, which heated up the stones,
All around the fire ring, were relics made of bones.
Then I crawled into the lodge, still hearing chants outside,
The water from the steam, was running down the hide.

Then the chanting stopped, no sound was heard at all,
Then all at once I heard, the spirits start to call.
I felt the evil in me, start moving all about,
I knew that it was eager, to find its own way out.

The evil spirit left me, like a bird it flew around,
The instant it was gone, the silence was profound.
When I crawled out of that lodge, my faith was whole again,
My people were in smiles, they knew I've shed my sin.

The sweat lodge it had saved me and washed away the bad,
Refilled my heart with good, just like I've always had.
My face it really shined, it had a special glow,
While I was sitting on a rock, carving my new bow.

Little Things

Enjoy the things around you, each and every day,
All of you enjoy, the time on earth you stay.
The hourglass is filling, the sand it quickly falls,
Little voices in you, say that heaven calls.

Things you have around you, some you've yet to see,
In your eyes you'll notice, your living wild and free.
Life is more than shiny things, or your banking worth,
My how time does quickly fly, since our precious birth.

Friends you have around you, take them on your trails,
Because of you they'll live, a life with open sails.
Each of us we matter, each and every one,
Day by day enjoy it, while living on the run.

The days are surely numbered, before our final part,
Sun can shine forever if your living from your heart.
Set out on adventure, you'll see just what I mean,
Is the life within you, saying set me free?

An eagle in the air, or just a passing smile,
Ending is for certain, so walk that extra mile.
To live within your world, as life was meant to be,
A feeling you will cherish, happy as can be.

Day will turn to dark, just to rise again,
You can spend your time, like leaves upon the wind.
Will you please just try it, and grab life by the horns,
Never will you look back, on a life so full of thorns.

Live to see the little things, and lend a helping hand,
Again, I wish you well, all my online friends.
See you in the mountains, somewhere along the trails,
while living midst the little things, oh the stories you can tell.

A Teardrop and A Smile

Been waiting on this special day, now birthing her first child,
She wears within a baby's cry, a teardrop and a smile.
For years we have been apart, divided by the miles,
I lay my eyes upon and shed, a teardrop and a smile.

I know your life is over, you have struggled for a while,
Knowing you are in heaven I'll wear, a teardrop and a smile.
Words spoken in a foster home, by an orphan child,
Are you my Dad? Was asked, I wore a teardrop and a smile.

I knew my life was over, out in the desert wild,
Then with a humble heart I wore, a teardrop and a smile.
Please go into the world, and help a needy child,
Then you can be the one to wear, a teardrop and a smile.

Courage

Tis not the bright of the midnight sun,
Dark of a moonless night has come.
Fear not what lurks within the night,
Shadows will fade far from your sight.

Strength arises from inner Self,
Courage that rests on a dusty shelf,
Of one's inner soul shall trust,
Remove the courage, blow off the dust.

Dark evils that lie within the night,
Will step aside, your path will light,
meek no more, subsides in you.
Brave the darkness, you travel through.

Tis morning rays, upon your trail,
Courage, strength and faith prevail.
Step aside, dark world down under,
Courage rings, pure sounds of thunder.

Fear not my friend, believe in yourself,
Find your courage, dust off your shelf.

Summer

In the cooling mountain breeze,
Under dancing aspen leaves,
I walk alone.

No worries for me,
Living life free,
Before summers gone.

Miracle in The Desert

I ride within the desert south, careless on the wind,
Sun is setting, evening falls, enchantment as my friend.
I lay my tiresome soul, recharging as I rest,
Evil lurked around me, in fear I grab my chest.

The evil it has found me, there in the desert sand,
The air around me thickens, I was a dying man.
In pain I start my battle, beneath a desert moon,
Death was getting closer; my time was very soon.

My Friends and family watched, helpless in their stance,
Me I fought my battle, with a truly little chance.
When some help arrived, medics sent from God,
With a grunt they lift me, up from that desert sod.

My memory fades away, beneath that desert sky,
They take me to some Angels, on wings with them I fly.
Wires and hoses abound me, not knowing how I lay,
Doc he tells my family, he gives me one more day.

That is when it happened, God placed his loving hand,
And helped me fight my battle, there in that arid land.
When I awoke from stillness, family looked upon,
A miracle in the desert, they thought that I had gone.

The desert sun is rising, I start my life anew,
Gods helping hand was with me, he's also there for you.
My days are very special, for me the sun shines bright,
Because of one great miracle, on a moonlit desert night.

TIME

Each day is a gift, a blessing blessed with time,
Make the best of each short day and let your happiness shine.
We never know from day to day, if this one is our last,
Slow down and smell the roses, try not to live so fast.

Seems we want to live so fast, in everything we do,
Take the time to stop and cherish, the things surrounding you.
In the big ole city, or near a babbling brook,
It doesn't matter where you live, just take the time to look.

You just might be amazed, with everything you see,
Dew drops on the roses, a beautiful lone tall tree.
This world is full of pleasures, if you only take the time,
To slow your pace to look at them and let their beauty shine.

Take the time to smile at others, and let your happiness grow,
Always be genuine and never put on a show,
Enjoy the small things in your life, with each passing minute,
Cause someday time will continue on, only without you in it.

Homely Dreams

I'm Standing in a special canyon, with cliffs on either side,
The sky has narrowed high above, White clouds are drifting by.
They're Shining in the canyon, beyond them cobalt blue,
As I rest upon this rock, my thoughts are tuned on you.

Even though we've never met, I've known you for a while,
Just Thinking of your beauty, it always makes me smile.
That's what keeps me going, when my trails are mighty long,
While Hiking in the canyons, I listen to natures songs.

On Farther down the canyon, the cliffs are closing in,
The stream in which I follow, disappears around the bend.
A chipmunk stops and stares at me, upon a rock ahead,
His mouth is full of pine needles, I'm sure they're for his bed.

I finally reached the special spot, the stream just falls away,
I'm Standing atop a waterfall, below me water sprays.
My trail has end, I look around, this place of serenity,
I feel that she is here somewhere, just staring right at me.

I know that in her beauty, I'll have a steady gaze,
While thoughts of her abound me, I know I'll be amazed.
Then suddenly, a bush just moved, shaken by a squirrel,
Under it, alas we meet, I smiled at a Homely Girl.

Near the Waters

A snowflake drifts in silence, upon the winter air,
It's journey quiet and peaceful, no worries to somewhere.
High above the mountain peaks, it drifts in black of night,
Gently falling, often changing, its course of where to lite.

Life's much like a snowflake, that drifts in mountains high,
It has its ups and downs, though someday it will die.
It's journey will be over, it's life will rest below,
Upon a padded blanket, of pure white mountain snow.

Our journey to the blanket, a life like drifting snow,
Our winds will someday fade, our time will melt and go.
So, live your life in happiness, embrace your winter winds,
Share the peace within you, before your snowflake ends.

The warmer days will soften, your mountain snows abound,
Like it you'll be a River and flow to lower ground.
Though once a flying wonder, a silent mountain snow,
Now way down in the valley, it's lovely river flows.

Along the rushing river, lush grass and flowers grow,
Beauty in abundance, because of mountain snows.
For you, a place of beauty, as equal does await,
The beauty near the waters, beyond our heaven's gate.

Good Ole Pal

Jdiggins spring awaits you, right around the bend,
Just a little longer, then chase your dreams within.
Remember while your chasing, I am wishing you the best,
Gold and jewels await you, hidden in an old-world chest.

If you find the special spot, and wear a marvel gaze,
Do not forget your good ole pal, here on the poetry page.

A Note to Corona Virus

You were born upon a distant soil,
You have crossed a mighty span.
Bringing grief and turmoil,
To spread across our lands.

But in your deadly rave,
You have made a great mistake.
This is the home of braves,
Your evil we will not take.

This is just a warning,
You best tuck tail and run.
No need to wait till morning,
Your evil here is done!

We will distance from our friends,
You will have nowhere to go.
Until your evil ends,
Our courage we will show.

So now you have had your warning,
Your evil we will not take.
We will not bow down in mourning,
Our freedom we will take.

We live red, white and blue,
Our Flag has never fell,
There is no half-mast for you,
We will we send you back to hell.

Home

We all come into this world, in a different time and place,
The one thing that we have in common, we share this beautiful space.
Notice all the little things, in our space we call earth,
Cause sometimes it's the smallest things, that have the greatest worth.

To some real beauty lies within, a skyscraper standing tall,
To others it's the sounds of serenity, in a remote little waterfall.
To others its more simple, small steps pattering down the hall,
Or maybe it's a grandchild, who just hit their first tee ball.

Maybe that first haircut, scared to sit real still,
To place within an envelope, and tightly press the seal.
Beauty comes in many forms, many shapes and sizes,
Take the time to notice them and enjoy all earths prizes.

God knew what he was doing, when he built this home we share,
Take care of it for years to come, to show him how much we care.
If I could pass one word of advice, to each and every man,
Love your neighbor, forgive a sinner, and thank God we have this land!

Canasta

I see you playing canasta, you said so CindyM,
Been a while since I have played, care if I join in?
You say your waters gone for now, soon it will be wet.
Then your journey can resume, on you I'll place my bet.

They say a joker brings good luck, kind of like a 4-leaf clover.
Hold it tightly close to you, once played the game is over.
If you look upon the" chest", I know you'll wear a grin,
Returning a turquoise bracelet, to the master Forrest Fenn.

If that happens, just promise me CindyM,
Gently break the news to us, your many online friends!

Tomorrow

The winds of time, blow quickly by,
Life's leaves of color fall.
Slumber Grey across the skies,
A chill with distant calls.

Your soul it has a window,
With frost upon its panes.
It stops the winds that blow,
Outside that call your name.

A fire that burns within you,
Has a warm and steady glow.
It'll help you through life's venue,
If tended as you grow.

But if your fires not tended,
And you fire it softly fades.
You'll know your time has ended,
With choices you have made.

So, while your winds are blowing,
And your cozy as can be.
Live your life while showing,
Others your warm and free.

Don't live your life in sadness,
Don't live within your sorrow,
Live your life in happiness,
Because your never promised tomorrow.

Indian Rain

While laying on my deer skin bed, the rain outside it falls,
It's tapping on my teepee roof; it's heard by me and all.
With interlocking fingers, placed behind my head,
My thoughts are free to roam, while laying here in bed.

My mind it slowly drifts away, to a time not long ago,
Before these springtime rains, the mountains still had snow.
My family they were hungry, our food was running out,
Time to do some hunting, that's what our life's about.

I tried and tried to find some food, but nothing day by day,
Walking farther from my village, I hunted as I strayed.
I couldn't ignore my hunger, my family they need fed,
Where are all the animals, kept dancing in my head.

At an open meadow, I knelt down on one knee,
With my bow in hand, I was ready as can be.
Then I see some movement, there on the other side,
The meadow I then skirted, with quietness in my stride.

When I reached the other side, a lone wapiti stood,
I drew my bow to try, to take him if I could.
I killed the lone wapiti, I'm so thankful I have meat,
Enough to feed my family, for many, many weeks.

I know my prayers were answered, my family feels the same,
Right then I knew we'd make it, to see these springtime rains.
As I'm listening to the rain, it fades away and stops,
Nothing now but silence, looking at my teepee top.

I think the rain is over now, I think I'll peek outside,
Then I grabbed my teepee door, made of mule deer hide.
I noticed how the sunshine, gives my home a glow,
Outside against a darkened sky, I see a huge rainbow.

Fennboree Family Reunion

Somewhere in the mountains, just north of Santa Fe,
The wind it softly blows, the trees they gently sway.
Family here will gather, even though we are not kin,
To celebrate adventures, because of Forrest Fenn.

Patiently I await, for my family to arrive,
The doodles they are hung, in hopes to win a prize.
Tom he's working hard, the smoke begins to lift,
Cynthia bless her soul, she's too a treasured gift.

Desertphile and Dal, they quietly walk around,
While a treasure map is drawn, with chalk upon the ground.
Then they start arriving, my family one by one,
Fennboree of 17, for me has now begun.

In case you didn't make it, our family I'll explain,
Each a special person, I only knew by name.
Jdiggins she arrives, a smile from ear to ear,
Then the voice of spallies, softly caught my ear.

Ken from down in Georgia, nice as he could be,
Together we sat and talked, beneath an aspen tree.
Nearindianajones and Keri, family now of mine,
Thank you for your smiles and giving me your time.

Fred Y he took the time, to make a game for kin,
Kids are tossing washers, trying to make them in.
Jimbo he is talking, to others by the wall,
While Alex with his camera, pics he takes of all.

So many now arriving, I can't keep up the pace,
Iron will he has his pies, a smile upon my face.
Seattlesullivan you're the man, research 101,
A backpack full of notes, since you first begun.

As my family mingles, Forrest he arrives,
Mildew on his head, and Shiloh by his side.
Greeting family one by one, he mingles right on in,
A smile as big as ours, upon the face of him.

Even though I'm trying, words just can't explain,
The pictures and the words are really not the same.
It was heaven in the mountains, everyone just glowed,
The Love within our family, from everybody showed.

If you didn't get to make it, to Fennboree this time,
Save the date for next year, I'll meet you in the pines.
Believe me when I say this and hear me when I say,
There's magic in the mountains, somewhere north of Santa Fe.

Given Time

I think today I will look.
Into my mirror bright and bold.
Looking for my final hook,
Seeing what my day beholds.

My mirror shows an autumn breeze,
Leaves falling in the wind.
Thank you, friend, for reminding me.
I say that with a grin.

In my mirror I also see,
A light that brightly shines.
On Friends like you, reminding me.
To enjoy my given time.

Fall Rainbow

Brisk winds of fall, setting in, to rest upon the leaves,
The green of summer, turns to gold, now floating in the breeze.
Orange, red and yellow, shining boldly in the sun,
But only for a little while, now fall has surely sprung.

While walking through the woodlands, admiring all the color,
The little chipmunks that I see, prepare their winter cover.
Just like all the other animals, hustling all around,
Trying to make their house a home before snow hits the ground.

Soon these woodlands will be covered, with a winter blanket of white,
The trees that bare the colors of fall, will be gone and out of sight.
Take the time and find a trail, and walk into the breeze,
Admire the colors fall has for you, there shining in the trees.

Hustle and bustle, our lives we live, always on the go,
Sometimes we forget the beauty, mother nature she does show.
You will not be sorry, for the time that you will spend,
Beneath the colors of the fall, that soon will surely end.

Your face will proudly show it, it will have a special glow,
Your heart will warmly feel it, as you visit Gods Rainbow.

Someday

Live out your given life,
For treasures still untold.
Today will soon pass by,
Dream what your future holds.

For those who live in hurry,
Tomorrow will be gone.
Love not in a scurry,
For paths you walk upon.

Life is yours get ready,
Rejoice along your way.
For if your slow and steady,
Eternity waits someday.

Match

My candle burns low,
In the darkness I will be,
Feeling for a match.

Dreams

Believe in which your soul does hark,
In dreams your heart is light.
You and only you can start,
And spread your wings in flight.

Make your nights of slumber rest,
Your solemn thought today.
Dreams within your only best,
Become your lighted way.

Reality is sometimes cruel,
Live in your dreams, that give.
My wish for you, a life that's full,
Friends take your time and "Live".

Tailing Streamers

I dream a dream of dreamers,
Magic filled my peaceful night.
A light with tailing streamers,
Glaring back at me so bright.

In that magic minute,
Nothing seemed as real,
Alone I stared upon it,
The warmness I could feel.

I see a man before me,
On a peaceful desert rock.
Navajo he seems to be,
I heard him as he talked.

Softly in his spirit voice,
Words he shared with me.
Helping is an act of choice,
Every soul it has a need.

Right your wrongs my friend,
Eternity waits for you.
Don't waste it till the end,
Relive your soul renewed.

Even in my solemn dreams,
Amidst my peaceful night.
My vision of the man it seems,
So, warming and so bright.

Live on, all you dreamers,
Imagination is the key,
Vision lights with tailing streamers,
Every dream you'll live to be.

Hope

My journey's end, not twice but three,
Yet still you hear, my words to thee.
When at the end, of life's short rope,
There is a knot, a glimmer of hope.

Words of Kindness

Words of kindness, spoke from within,
Float in the soul, like leaves on wind.
DU you have spoken, I hear you my friend,
So, see ya till next time, we'll soon meet again.

Chasing Dreams

Dreams within your inner self,
Are sometimes left suppressed.
To languish on your inner shelf,
Be aware of where they rest.

Chased by some, with wanderlust,
But left by those who dwell.
The dreams that sit and gather dust,
Reward no empty shell.

Is this the way it's meant to be,
Within a dreaming heart?
The treasure lies inside of the,
Journeys go, now start.

So, chase your dusty dreams anew,
If you dare to live a life.
Captured in your journey to,
Release your world of strife.

Them journeys that you give your heart,
And rewards to keep oneself,
Chase away a world so dark,
Again, go chase yourself.

Mountain Night

Deep within a wilderness, I rest upon a log,
With nightfall closing on me, sounds of nearby frogs.
The sky above is clear, the stars begin to peek,
I listened to the stillness; a voice begins to speak.

Softly as a whisper, but clear as if it's near,
A voice so warm and soothing, falls upon my ears.
Alarmed I look around, alone no one in sight,
His spirit it then whispers, within the mountain night.

He said he was Apache, from many moons ago,
He roamed this very land, till time for him to go.
He soared with mighty eagles, he rode upon the wind,
His spirit as he left here, a proud man way back then.

He said he's left me something, made by his own hands,
His voice I then followed, through the thick and wooded land.
A cliff is now before me, he says to cross the stream,
Carefully I managed, a cave before me seen.

A cave with painted symbols, my light it shines within,
Amazed with what's before me, with whispers now from him.
Upon the dim lit ground, a pot of hardened clay,
Pictures all around it, as if in some display.

His spirit it then left me, as quickly as it came,
I didn't get to thank him, or even get his name.
And with my pot in hand, amazed at such a sight,
I'm thankful for his visit, here in this mountain night.

Around the Family Table

Sitting here reflecting, on Thanksgivings of the past,
Cherishing all the memories made, memories that will last.
Turkey thawing on the counter, and now Thanksgiving Eve,
Right beside the biggest ham, I believe I've ever seen.

My sister she is bringing, her good ole Mac & Cheese,
The stuffing made by brother, is sure enough to please.
Mashed potatoes creamy smooth, brought by my Uncle Dan,
Fresh made rolls all buttered, from my other sister Jan.

Pumpkin pie with cool whip, my niece said she would bring,
My wife's in charge of apple pie, it will make your taste buds sing.
Green beans wrapped in bacon, brought by my eldest son,
He always has an empty dish; they are loved by everyone.

I will have the turkey brown, ready for Grandpa Ken,
While carving he'll tell us stories, how hard life was back then.
My Nephew usually brings, a surprise that he whips up,
Not good in the kitchen, cooking mainly on his luck.

It will be a special day, when tomorrow does arrive,
The joining of my family, a break from busy lives.
To sit around the table, and enjoy a Thanksgiving dinner,
All the stories, all the smiles, where everyone is a winner.

There's so much I am thankful for, I know where I should start,
I will start by thanking God above, for my healthy beating heart.
For being right beside me, at a time that was so grim,
Because of God, I write these words, I owe it all to him.

I'm thankful for my family, who never left my side,
I know I cannot repay them, no matter how I try.
The sun comes up, the sun goes down, each and every day,
For life I am so thankful, that is all that I can say.

Take some time, on Thanksgiving Day, give thanks to God above,
For all that you are thankful for and thank him for his love.
Look around your table, just look and you will see,
Be thankful for the time you have, with your loving FAMILY.

Echoing Through Time

Native chants of way back then,
Can still be heard on prairie winds,
Echoing through time.

Their drums beat like a thunders boom,
So loud beneath the nightly moon,
Echoing through time.

Their spirits live beyond the light,
And chant within their world so bright,
Echoing through time.

Their chants and drums will never die,
Forever on the wind they'll always fly,
Echoing through time.

So, place your ear into the wind,
And listen for our native friends,
Echoing through time.

The day will come when we all will fly,
Our voice will drift in the same prairie sky,
Echoing through time.

So, when you hear the chanting start,
Embrace the sound within your heart,
Echoing through time.

Angel of The Mourning

Smoke it rises to the sky,
In a valley far below.
From fires within a native tribe,
Their home so long ago.

Teepees stand in numbers,
There on the valley floor.
Sun ends their morning slumber,
They start their daily chores.

From high above I gaze,
Upon their desert home.
A dim lit Smokey haze,
Although they now are gone.

In thought I am there with them,
Though many years have passed.
Spirits in the wind,
Have come to me at last.

Though gone, I can see them,
I hear their native chants.
I smell the Smokey winds,
From high above their camp.

A subtle voice is spoken,
Into my morning ears.
Her silence has been broken,
Though mute for many years.

Her ancient words were lovely,
There in the morning light.
She says someday she'll greet me,
Beyond my final flight.

Flowing Water

Warm fishing seasons, come and go,
Bright yellow leaves, then on to snow.
It warms the soul, removes the shiver,
Those memories made, upon the river,

Until the Bloom, of early spring,
And nature's call, begins to sing.
Those memories then, one can recall,
As fly rod hangs, upon the wall.

Until the Mayfly, hatch resumes,
A fireplace lights, a dim lit room.
Dreaming of the days much hotter,
And casting on, the flowing water.

Parting Ways

In the year of 1862, on a partly cloudy day,
Elders smoke their pipe, while children swim and play.
The winter it was long, now Summer's at our door,
Everyone is happy, upon our creek side shore.

Our hunters they're out hunting, for our daily meal,
Soon they will return, with them their daily kill.
Me I sit alone, across our little creek,
Just listening to the spirits, as they softly speak.

I notice as the years passed, with each new winter wind,
The boys of our camp have slowly turn to men.
Me I am an elder, like those upon the bank,
And To the mighty spirit, I give him all my thanks.

For many moons I've walked, upon this precious ground,
And now my legs are weak, my voice a softened sound.
My winters are now over, my time is very near,
The mighty heavens spirit, it whispers in my ear.

As I gaze across the creek, my heart is full of pride,
I'd live right here forever, beside this ole creek side.
I know it's time for me to do, what I was taught I should,
A tear rolls down my wrinkled face, as I walk into the woods.

Be Happy

You listen to your mind,
Only you can hear.
Live your life and shine,
Once you have shed your tear.

Do the things you love,
Whatever it may be.
It is a gift from up above,
Takes joyful eyes to see.

To others show your smiles,
Be happy while you do,
Happiness goes for miles,
But it starts right there with you.

Forever More

A door will open, a door will close,
A spirit flies, then off it goes.
On journey's to, a place unknown,
Where many spirits, before have flown.

To rest within, a place of shine,
Not measured by our Earthly time.
The past resumes, as once it was,
Rejoicing with, the ones we love.

No pain nor sorrow, within this place,
Just peaceful smiles, on every face.
Love and laughter, amongst old friends,
For eternity there, which has no end.

Prepare your spirit, for journeys new,
You hold the key, inside of you.
To fly within, this unlocked door,
Peace you'll have, forever more.

Goodbye

I too have lost an arrow high,
No time to say my last goodbye.
Upon the midday summer breeze,
It flew off through some distant trees.

Walking, looking, I thought I could,
Find it hiding, within the wood.
And very much to my surprise,
Alas I get to say goodbye.

Shade

I've seen the tree in which you speak, just this passing fall,
Standing so majestic, and proud to be so tall.
The man who came with ax in hand, looked at the tree and smiled,
I will build my home of brick, to shelter my wife and child.

Lowered his ax and turned away, to leave this beautiful place,
With a look of pleasure, bestowed upon his face.
The decision to let the tree stand tall, for everyone to see,
Thank you, man with ax, especially from me.

The next time you're out hiking, and you pass a lone tall tree,
Take the time to admire its limbs, standing so beautifully.
Even though it's just in passing, a moment of your time,
The tree will be forever blessed, to know you are so kind.

The tree will stand up taller, than it ever has before,
knowing that someone's admiring him, down at the forest floor.
You will not be sorry, for this little spec of time,
To let the tall tree show its grace, and let its beauty shine.

Thank you, man who took your ax, and went on quietly home,
I see you wife and children, they like their house of stone.
I know your happy to, with the choices you have made,
While you and family enjoy, your picnic in its shade.

Old Glory

Old glory is a symbol of our freedom we all share,
She proudly shows her stripes, while waving in the air.
She's carried in the battlefield, upon our soldiers' sleeve,
A symbol of our courage, to chase what we believe.

She waves across our country, shines red, white and blue,
A reminder of the soldiers, who died for me and you.
Old glory she has waved, tattered on front lines,
Though frazzled she continues, to let her colors shine.

Our founding fathers flew her, to show for which they stand,
Peace for each and every one, across our precious land.
So, on this day remember, the lives that many gave,
So, we can watch "Old Glory", as she gently waves.

Fear Not

Fear not, as I gaze into the clear night,
Great darkness behind, the stars ever bright.
Where a myriad of souls, before me they flew,
Embracing adventure, their journeys anew.

Brave is the soul, that travels to where,
No pain, no sorrow, up in the night air.
Fear it not, I'll be ever so bold,
Upon this great journey, whatever it holds.

While hanging my star, up high in the sky,
Peace will abound me; my spirit will fly.
Many will follow, in a terrible fright,
But for me I fear not, as I gaze in the night.

Behind

High upon a mountainside, extremely near the top,
Towering cliffs are rising, as if to never stop.
I sit within the solitude, alone with just my thoughts,
Seeking for the answers, lifelong I have sought.

The sky above is blue, white clouds are sparsely spread,
I rummage through my thoughts, that bounce within my head.
I gaze down in a valley, green from summer sun,
Carved by an ancient glacier, back when it all begun.

The juniper and pines, are scattered down below,
Five lakes I see below me, filled by melting snows.
I feel I sit in heaven, here on this mountain side,
A jumping doe just passed me, in search of where to hide.

And way down in the valley, there's movement near the scrub,
A black bear eating berries, along her stands her cub.
And high up in the sky, the eagle's soar around,
Continually they are searching, for movement on the ground.

The chipmunks scurry wildly, in search for winter beds,
Me I'm still in thought, for answers in my head.
This is when it happened, a cool wind starts to blow,
A voice of one Apache, from many years ago.

His spirit softly speaks, he knew that I was there,
He tells me he once breathed, this chilly mountain air.
He says to look below, my seat of flattened stone,
He said this was the mountain, he gladly called his home.

I looked below the rock, amazed at what I found,
A necklace made by him, just lying on the ground.
With his gift in hand, I hear him say goodbye,
Then his spirit left me, back into chilly skies.

The answers that I looked for, I found them on that day,
High upon a mountain, near trees that gently swayed.
It's not about the riches, that you can say are mine,
It's more about the gifts, you proudly leave behind.

I Wish

I wish I were a firefly,
Floating in the nighttime air.
Or maybe just a glow worm,
With my well-lit Dari-air.

Daydreams

I walk into a forest, I sit upon a rise,
Admiring all the beauty, that lay before my eyes.
The rays that filter through the trees, softly light the floor,
Chipmunks scurrying all about, doing their daily chores.

A hint of movement in the brush, quickly caught my eye,
A doe with her spotted fawn, came strolling slowly by.
No care at all, that I was there, she knew I meant no harm,
Just then a butterfly softly lit, careless upon on my arm.

It flies off, then I stand, to leave this heavenly place,
I start walking, off the rise, a smile upon my face.
The memories that I made that day, will last my whole life Long,
You too should walk into the forest and listen to natures song.

As I'm walking along the path, I hear a large stick break!
Then something grabs me by the shoulder and frightens me awake.
Just to realize, that I was dreaming because I dozed off asleep,
The oil change man, then said to me, "your keys are on the seat".

Slow Down

It's time to take it slow, each and every day,
Not to zip and go, like a Nascar on your way.
Who can take it slow? You asked while passing by.
You should someday know; you'll love it if you try.

Are the things around you, quickly flying past?
It's time to live life slower, not to live so fast.
Who wants their days to fly? not me, that's for sure.
They go quick enough; in slowness I'll endure.

Think about my words to you, the choice is yours to make.
You will see the beauty, as your life you slowly take.
Are you really living? Your throttle belongs to you.

Clearing My Head

close your eyes jdiggins, and open your heart,
You began winning, right from the start.
The day that the Chase, landed online,
Dreaming and adventures flooded our minds.

We have packed our bags, and traveled afar,
Enjoyed all the landscapes, we have seen from our car,
Climbed tall mountains, searched riverbeds too,
All these things are prizes for you.

Every person who has played this game from the start,
Has won their own prize deep in their heart,
Next adventure you take, please sit on a log,
Just think of the friends you made on this blog.

There's Amy, Mindy, Cloudcover too,
Not to mention there's Me and there's You,
Dal and Goof, Spallies so bold,
Let us not forget, oh pirates of Gold.

Too many to name, here on Dals blog,
But think of us all, while perched on your log.
See, jdiggins you have already won,
Now play the game and play it for fun.

Go out and search for treasures galore,
Then recharge yourself and do it some more,
The Chase is what it's really about,
The ups and the downs the ins and the outs.

If the gold you find while on your way,
Congrats to you I would quickly say,
But look around, 360 degrees,
There is your treasure, the rivers and trees.

Enjoy them jdiggins and everyone else too,
someday I am hoping that I will run into you.

somewhere Along the many trails up ahead,
Resting and thinking, just clearing my head.

HE

He came into this world, to die for you and me,
Causing lame to walk, causing blind to see.
He walked throughout the desert, roaming town to town,
Speaking words from heaven, in a lengthy woven gown.

Followed by believers, to hear his mighty voice,
He said we have a home, that's if we make the choice.
Through him a door is open, to a home as white as snow,
Large enough for all, who choose they want to go.

As he gained attention, word spread throughout the land,
Some they turned against him, this new messiah man.
the anger caught and bound him, and beat him with their whips,
Through the blood and torture, only grace fell from his lips.

They nailed him to a cross, to prove to every man,
That they would not accept, righteous in their land.
His blood was dark and red, with thorns around his head,
Believers knelt and prayed, for their messiah now was dead.

They placed him in a tomb and sealed it with a stone,
Guarded by some soldiers, who were pacing to and from.
Three days slowly passed, the stone was rolled away,
Just to find a robe, there where messiah laid.

Soldiers hit their knees, for they knew his words were true,
He opens up a door, to a home for me and you.
From that day on his love, spread throughout the lands,
He was a true messiah, with healing in his hands.

Many came with baskets, with fruit and special things,
And left them at the tomb, an offering to their king.
My friends please don't forget, how "HE" has paved the way,
Enjoy your time with family, on this awesome Easter Day.

Midnight

The other side of midnight, I often drift to dream,
Of those who's hour struck, 12 times ahead of me.
A place off in the future, a place where time stands still,
A place for grand reunions, a place I often steal.

The other side of midnight, so far, but yet so near,
Trekked by those before me, their chime I often hear.
Ringing in my memories, of days so long ago,
The laughter and the tears, before they had to go.

I wait, the clock is ticking, its pendulum is slow,
Can't wait to see your faces, beyond the midnights glow.
For now, I'll sit and listen and dream of such a sight,
When I make my final journey, into the midnight light.

And when I'm gone be happy, don't grieve for me I say,
For I have found that place, I dreamed of day to day,
I'll meet the past before me, I'll love in such a sight,
I too will know what lies, past the other side of midnight...

Alone

Alone I sit in nature's chatter,
I think about what really matters.
Will someday those who look on me,
Find what I already see?

Peace within my daily life,
Alone I face a world of strife.
I try to spread, what is oh so real,
Will others find, what I now feel?

Live on my friends, with lightened load,
In lush green gardens, of which you've sowed.
Peace abundant, awaits in there,
And comforts those, who really care.

Alone here in this gentle breeze,
I wait for all, in which I see.
Will others see while looking down,
Die with peace, like I have found?

In closing I must surely say,
Peace my friend's, the only way.

Old Home Place

Sunlight beams, through leaves of gold,

Brisk in air, chilly and cold.

Remote I stand, near tales of old,

Silence here, no stories told.

Rocks that rise, unto the sky,

No smell of smoke, just lonely I.

Forest floor, with raging vine,

Taking over, through midst of time.

Vines to cover, the rocks of home,

Time did win, now all is gone.

Circle of rock, of old open well,

Bucket of rust, decayed where it fell.

Silence it soothes, my heart as I roam,

At an old place, my ancestors called home.

Sun sets lower, with each passing minute,

Chill is much colder, but proud that I'm in it.

I leave with feeling, whole once again,

Replenished by family, ancestors of kin.

Before I leav , this place that I roam,

Thanks to my family, for calling me home.

The sun is now set, dark moving in fast,

Please take the time, to visit your past.

Your heart wont regret it, no not for a minute,

Let the past come alive, let family back in it.

In silent repose, your old home place waits,

For you to come visit, with smile on your face.

Dark is now here, a single owl hoots,

Replenish your soul, go visit your roots.

406   *James Bynum*

So Long Ago

Before the Spanish came, into the northern lands,
Natives lived in harmony, across the arid sands.
They also lived-in peace, across the mountains wide,
From snow caps to the desert, the Indians lived with pride.

Their daily life was hardened, hunting for their meals,
The hunters fed the tribes, with their daily kills.
Women made their pots of clay, to carry water in,
Children carried firewood, that's how it was back then.

The braves they gave protection and sometimes gave their life,
The elders gave their wisdom, craftsmen made their knifes.
The land it gave them healing, in many different herbs,
Spirits above would listen, to their native words.

They lived their life in harmony, and each would do their part,
The pride within the Indians, sowed deep within their hearts.
With their nightly fires aglow, the embers rising red,
They'd whisper to the heavens, before they went to bed.

With the early morning light, they'd do it all again,
Living their life in peace, that's how it was back then.
Maybe we could learn, from the long-lost Indians,
And live our lives in harmony, just like our native friends.

If each of us would take the time, and do our selfless part,
Then we could live in peace, with pride within our hearts.
To all my native friends, who lived so long ago,
You are not forgotten, I thought you ought to know.

Should I Say Goodbye

Should I say goodbye? Should I blow you a kiss?
Should I wave really big, to the ones I'll miss?
Whichever the choice, the results are the same,
My friends they'll become, a memory by name.

Memories in time, so lovely and bright,
We laughed and we cried, we talked through the night.
We helped out our friends, during troublesome times,
We shared our big hearts, through our words of rhyme.

Jdiggins is where, my memory begins,
Her hug when she saw me, her biggest of grins.
And Spallies beside her, with her hat on her head,
Smiling and joking, at all that we said.

Then Jenny Kyle hugged me, so many around,
Ken Up from Georgia and others abound.
Special things happened, in the darkest of light,
As nearindianajones and I, shook hands in the night.

Dal he's a fun one and Desertphile too,
Almost as fun, as the large Texas crew.
There's Brooke and there's Covert, he says he's the one,
To many to mention, but God it was fun!

There was Tom Terrific, in his shady ole hat,
While PauleyT and others, sat near the back.
And Anna, whew, now what can I say?
The sweetest of sweet, on any ole day.

There's to many to mention, that I've met face to face,
But There's many I haven't, shook hands in this chase.
CuriousGeorge, he's a good Nikan of mine,
Pdenver's so sweet, to all of mankind.

There's 4rest4fend and wwwamericana too,
Amber and BigOnus, with hearts big as two.
SuzyS and others, like Hank and his rhyme,
Oh, and Lisa Cesari, she's the kindest of kind.

And also, there's a friend, I call JDA,
My words can't express, but I'll meet him someday.
If your name is not mentioned, your loved just the same,
I've so many new friends, I've loaded my brain.

But soon you will all, be a memory of mine,
But forever you'll last, till the end of my time.
I hope and I pray, for each of you all,
A life full of blessings and happiness for ya'll.

So, I won't say goodbye, it's so hard to do,
I won't blow a kiss, to my friends such as you.
I'm not waving big, you're not going nowhere,
In my heart you'll remain, you'll always be there.

If you want to chime in, or just sit and chat,
My emails below, you know where I'm at.
My heart feels really heavy, I'm sure yours does too,
But I promise you friends, there's journeys anew.

We'll make it alright, after this time that we're blue,
Enjoy the little things, as you try something new.
So, farewell for now, until our trails cross again,
I guess until next time… I'll see ya my friends.

Until Next Time... See Ya...

CPSIA information can be obtained
at www.ICGtesting.com
Printed in the USA
LVHW060856210521
688043LV00010B/848